TOXIC
SUPERFOODS
COOKBOOK

100+ Delicious Recipes for Oxalate Overload Recovery and overall wellbeing

Valerie R. Johnson

Copy Right Page

Table of Content

Introduction

Welcome to the entrance of transformation—where every page of the *"Toxic Superfoods Cookbook"* is an invitation to a life of robust health, taste, and fulfillment. In the rhythm of everyday life, we often confront problems that impair our well-being, and for many, oxalate overload becomes an unforeseen hurdle on the way to optimal health.

The Importance of Oxalate Balance in Maintaining Optimal Health

An often-underappreciated aspect of diet, regulating oxalates is becoming more and more important in the complex dance of sustaining overall health and wellness. When their levels are carefully regulated, oxalates—naturally occurring chemicals present in a variety of foods—can significantly contribute to our overall well-being.

- **Knowing Oxalates:** Many plant-based foods naturally contain oxalates, which enhance their flavor, texture, and nutritional value. Although oxalates do not have any intrinsic detrimental properties, an excess of them in the body might cause problems, thus it is important to consume them in moderation.

- **The Connection to Kidney Health**: The possible harm that oxalates may do to the kidneys is one of the main justifications for their balance. Kidney stones can develop when the body's oxalate levels get too high and solidify. People can reduce their risk of kidney stones and promote the general health of this important organ by eating an appropriate amount of oxalate.

- **Gut Health and Nutrient Absorption:** Oxalates may also interfere with the digestive system's ability to absorb minerals by interacting with them. Maintaining adequate nutrient absorption and enabling the body to absorb the most nutrients possible from the foods we consume depend on finding a balance in our oxalate consumption.

- **Inflammation and Oxalate Sensitivity:** Inflammation and discomfort may be exacerbated in certain people by an oxalates imbalance. Reducing the likelihood of inflammatory reactions in the body and enhancing digestive comfort need an understanding of and management of oxalate sensitivity.

The delicate balance between oxalates and calcium metabolism is important for bone health. People may help maintain strong, healthy bones by regulating their consumption of oxalate, protecting themselves from dangerous imbalances that could impair bone density.

Techniques for Harmonious Oxalate Balance:

Making well-considered dietary decisions is essential to achieving a harmonious oxalate balance. This entails determining which foods are high in oxalate and combining a range of low-oxalate substitutes. Certain cooking methods, such soaking and boiling, can also be used to lower the amount of oxalate in food.

Motivating Health-Conscious Decisions:

Maintaining an appropriate balance of oxalates is more than simply making dietary changes; it's about taking the initiative to make decisions that are health-conscious. People may take charge of their own health by being aware of and actively balancing oxalates in their everyday lives, whether they are managing pre-existing diseases or taking preventative actions.

To sum up, the importance of maintaining an equilibrium of oxalates for good health cannot be stressed. It's a complex strategy that calls for awareness, thoughtful decision-making, and a dedication to general wellbeing. People may take a critical step toward encouraging a better and more balanced lifestyle by adopting this holistic viewpoint.

Chapter 1: Understanding Oxalates:

What are Oxalates?

Naturally occurring substances, oxalates are present in many plant-based diets. They are a part of the broader group of substances called oxalic acid. Many fruits, vegetables, nuts, seeds, cereals, and even certain drinks contain oxalates in various amounts.

Oxalates are used by plants for a variety of reasons. They aid in the defensive mechanisms of the plant against pests and herbivores and are involved in the control of calcium levels in the plant. On the other hand, oxalates may combine with minerals like calcium and magnesium in the human body to produce crystals.

The accumulation of oxalates crystals in the body, especially in the kidneys, where they can mix with calcium to create kidney stones, is a possible cause for worry. For this reason, those who are at risk of kidney stones or who have specific medical problems may want to limit their consumption of oxalate.

It's crucial to remember that not all oxalates are created equal, and that an individual's general health and the sort of oxalates they consume can determine how they affect their health. Oxalates may cause higher sensitivity in some persons than in others.

Commonly, foods with increased oxalates content include:

- Swiss chard with spinach
- green beets
- Rosemary
- Nuts and seeds—particularly sesame and peanut—
- Hazelnut Tea
- Certain berries, such raspberries and blackberries
- Sweet potatoes with okra etc.

Certain cooking techniques, such boiling and soaking, can aid in lowering the oxalate content of food. A healthy intake of oxalates and other nutrients can also be achieved by eating a diverse range of foods in a well-balanced diet.

To find the best nutritional options for their particular requirements, those with certain health concerns—like renal problems—must consult with medical practitioners or certified dietitians.

Health Impacts of Oxalate Overload

The overabundance of oxalates in the body, or oxalate overload, can have a number of negative health effects, especially for those who are more vulnerable to oxalate-related problems. The following are a few possible health effects of oxalate overload:

Kidney Stones:

Kidney stones are the most well-known adverse health effect of oxalate excess. Kidney stones can develop as a result of oxalates combining with calcium to create crystals, which can subsequently collect. These stones may need to be removed by a doctor and can be quite painful.

Gastrointestinal Distress:

For those who are sensitive, too many oxalates may be a factor in digestive problems. This might involve symptoms including bloating, discomfort, or pain in the abdomen, especially in those who have irritable bowel syndrome (IBS) or other digestive disorders.

Nutrient Absorption Interference:

Oxalates have the ability to bind to minerals, such as magnesium and calcium, to produce compounds that the body absorbs more slowly. This disruption of the absorption of nutrients may affect the state of one's nutrition overall and lead to shortages in some vital minerals.

Inflammation and Joint Pain:

High oxalate levels have been linked to joint discomfort or inflammation in certain people. This is especially important for people with specific inflammatory diseases or those who are prone to oxalate sensitivity.

Possible Sensitivity to Oxalate:

It's possible that some people are more susceptible to oxalates than others. Skin rashes, joint discomfort, and other allergic-type responses are some of the signs that might indicate oxalate sensitivity. To reduce the negative effects on health, oxalate sensitivity must be identified and managed.

Issues with Bone Health:

Excessive oxalates may affect calcium metabolism, even though the link between oxalates and bone health is complicated. This may, in certain circumstances, have an impact on bone density and exacerbate problems relating to bones.

Elevated Production of Oxalate in the Body:

Rarely, oxalates may be produced by the body naturally, which would raise blood levels. Hypercalcaluria is the name of the disorder that can lead to kidney stones and other health issues.

It's crucial to remember that not everyone will suffer from these health effects, and that each person's symptoms may vary in intensity. Furthermore, many people can withstand a certain amount of oxalates without experiencing any side effects. It is best to speak with a medical expert or a qualified dietitian if you have any concerns about oxalate overload or associated health issues.

They can offer individualized advice based on each person's needs and health circumstances.

Identifying High-Oxalate Foods

Understanding and recognizing high-oxalate foods are essential cornerstones in the complex web of dietary choices for those managing kidney stone, oxalate sensitivity, or other associated health issues.

This is a brief guide to help you in your search for accuracy when it comes to identifying foods high in oxalates:

1. Refer to Reliable Sources:

Start your journey with trustworthy resources including nutrition databases, medical literature, and advice from medical specialists. Equip oneself with knowledge that serves as the foundation for oxalate awareness.

2. Become Knowledgeable on Typical Offenders:

Be prepared by learning about typical foods that have high levels of oxalates. Nuts, seeds, chocolate, spinach, Swiss chard, and certain berries are common additions.

Being aware of these offenders gives you the ability to choose your diet with knowledge.

3. Examine Nutrition Labels Carefully:

Become a label investigator. Pay close attention to the oxalate content listed on nutrition labels when purchasing packaged foods. Even though not all labels contain this information, using discernment will guarantee that the decisions you make support your oxalate management objectives.

4. Utilize Databases Oxalate:

Examine online oxalate databases that are devoted to provide comprehensive details on the oxalate concentration of different foods. These are excellent resources for accurate meal planning.

5. Expert Cooking Methods:

Take use of the power of culinary techniques. You can minimize the amount of oxalates in some foods by boiling, soaking, and leaching, which will give you more culinary options.

6. Watch Out for Drinks High in Oxalate:

Take caution when navigating the beverage environment. Tea and other fruit juices are examples of beverages that can greatly increase the amount of oxalate consumed. Here, making thoughtful decisions is essential to striking a balance.

7. Keep an eye on portion sizes:

Recall that moderation is crucial. Even while certain meals could contain a lot of oxalates, controlling portion sizes enables you to enjoy tastes without going against your dietary goals.

8. Document Your Gastronomic Adventure:

Think of maintaining a food journal. This is your compass, letting you track how much oxalate you consume each day, see trends, and make the best dietary decisions for your health.

9. Recognize Personal Sensitivity:

Accept the individuality of your physique. Understand that each person's sensitivity to oxalates varies. Be mindful of your body's reactions and adjust your diet accordingly.

10. Look for Expert Advice:

Improve your oxalate control plan by consulting certified dietitians or other medical specialists. Their knowledge guarantees a customized strategy that fits your dietary requirements and health objectives.

Set off on your path with assurance, knowing how to choose between meals that support your health and those that might require more investigation. Accurately recognizing foods rich in oxalate requires a commitment to your health and vitality, not merely a dietary decision.

Chapter 2: Appetizers That Heal:

Oxalate-Conscious Starters

Stuffed Mushrooms with Feta and Spinach

Description: Savor the tasty pairing of spinach and feta nestled within delicately roasted mushrooms for a delectable and low-oxalate appetizer.

Prep time: 20 minutes

Cooking time: 15 minutes

12 Serving

Ingredients:

- Twelve big mushrooms with removed stems
- One cup of freshly chopped spinach,
- half a cup of crumbled feta cheese,
- two cloves of minced garlic,
- and two teaspoons of olive oil
- Add pepper and salt to taste.
- For garnish, use fresh parsley.

Preparation:

1. Turn the oven on to 375°F, or 190°C.
2. Minced garlic should be cooked in olive oil in a skillet until aromatic.
3. Cook the chopped spinach in the pan until it wilts.
4. Combine the crumbled feta, salt, and pepper with the sautéed spinach in a bowl.

5. Put a little of the spinach and feta mixture into each mushroom cap.
6. Bake the mushrooms for 15 minutes, or until they are soft, in a preheated oven.
7. Serve with fresh parsley as a garnish.

Avocado and Cucumber Salsa Cups

Description: These cucumber cups packed with a spicy avocado salsa are a great way to start any oxalate-conscious meal. They offer a refreshing rush of flavors.

Prep time: 20 minutes

Serving Size: Yields fifteen cups.

Ingredients:

- Three big cucumbers
- Two avocados, cut up
- Half a cup of cherry tomatoes
- 1/4 cup finely chopped red onion; 1/4 cup chopped cilantro; 1 lime, juiced;
- Add pepper and salt to taste.

Preparation:

1. After peeling, slice the cucumbers into rounds that are one inch thick.
2. Scoop out the center of each round of cucumber using a small spoon or melon baller to form a cup.
3. Diced avocados, cherry tomatoes, red onion, cilantro, lime juice, salt, and pepper should all be combined in a bowl.
4. Fill each cucumber cup with a spoonful of avocado salsa.

5. Place on a dish for serving, and savor.

Walnut and Roasted Red Pepper Dip

Description: Savor a decadent and velvety walnut and roasted red pepper dip accompanied by crunchy, oxalate-tolerant vegetable chips.

Prep time: 15 minutes

Cooking time: 20 minutes

Serving Size: Eight pieces

Ingredients:

- Roasted and peeled two big red bell peppers
- One cup of roasted walnuts
- Garlic cloves, two
- 1/4 cup of olive oil
- One-third cup lemon juice
- Add pepper and salt to taste.
- dippers made of several vegetables (cucumber, carrot, celery)

Preparation:

1. Roasted red peppers, toasted walnuts, garlic, olive oil, and lemon juice should all be combined in a food processor.
2. Mix until homogeneous. To taste, add more salt and pepper.
3. Pour the dip into a dish for serving.
4. Accompany with celery, carrot sticks, and cucumber slices.

Roll-Ups with Goat Cheese and Zucchini

Description: These exquisite zucchini roll-ups, packed with a light and tangy goat cheese combination, will elevate your appetizer game.

Prep time: 20 minutes

Cooking time: 10 minutes

Serve Size: Enough to Make 16 Roll-Ups

Ingredients:

- Two medium zucchini, cut lengthwise into thin slices
- Goat cheese, four ounces
- One tablespoon of toasted pine nuts and two teaspoons of freshly chopped basil
- One tsp of lemon zest
- Add pepper and salt to taste.

Preparation:

1. Turn on the medium heat and preheat a grill or grill pan.
2. To make zucchini slices soft, grill them for one to two minutes on each side.
3. After removing, let them cool.
4. Combine goat cheese, roasted pine nuts, chopped basil, lemon zest, salt, and pepper in a bowl.
5. On each slice of zucchini, apply a thin coating of the goat cheese mixture.
6. Using toothpicks, secure the rolled pieces.
7. Place in a serving dish and proceed to serve.

Stuffed peppers with quinoa and roasted vegetables

Description: These quinoa and roasted vegetable-stuffed tiny peppers are a delightful and healthy oxalate-conscious beginning that will leave you feeling full and satisfied.

Prep time: 30 minutes

Cooking time: 25 minutes

Serving Size: Yields 20 filled bell peppers.

Ingredients:

- One cup cooked quinoa, ten tiny bell peppers cut in half and seeded
- 1 cup chopped cherry tomatoes,
- 1 diced zucchini,
- 1 diced yellow squash, and 1/2 cup finely chopped red onion
- Two tsp of olive oil
- One tsp of dehydrated oregano
- Add pepper and salt to taste.
- For garnish, use fresh parsley.

Preparation:

1. Turn the oven on to 375°F, or 190°C.
2. Cherry tomatoes, zucchini, yellow squash, and red onion should all be combined with olive oil, oregano, salt, and pepper in a bowl.

3. Spread the combination of vegetables onto a baking sheet and roast for fifteen minutes.
4. Combine the cooked quinoa and the roasted veggies in a separate bowl.
5. Spoon the quinoa and veggie mixture into each half of the tiny peppers.
6. Bake the peppers for ten more minutes, or until they are soft.
7. Serve with fresh parsley as a garnish.

Stuffed Mushrooms with Spinach and Artichokes Dip

Description: These bite-sized appetizers are rich and oxalate-conscious, combining the flavors of a traditional spinach and artichoke dip with delicately roasted mushrooms.

Prep Time: 20 minutes

Cooking time: 20 minutes

Ingredients:

- 24 button mushrooms with the stems cut off
- 1 cup of defrosted, squeezed-dry frozen spinach
- 1 cup chopped canned artichoke hearts and 1/2 cup softened cream cheese
- 1/4 cup mustard
- 1/4 cup of Parmesan cheese, grated
- one minced garlic clove
- Add pepper and salt to taste.
- For garnish, use fresh parsley.

Preparation:

1. Turn the oven on to 375°F, or 190°C.
2. Thawed spinach, chopped artichoke hearts, cream cheese, mayonnaise, Parmesan cheese minced garlic, salt, and pepper should all be combined in a bowl.
3. Spoon the spinach and artichoke mixture into each mushroom cap.
4. Bake the mushrooms for 20 minutes, or until they are soft, in a preheated oven.
5. Serve with fresh parsley as a garnish.

Fig skewers dipped in balsamic glaze

Description: Savor the traditional tastes of caprese salad on skewers with a balsamic glaze for a colorful and fresh appetizer that is low in oxalate.

Prep Time: 15 minutes

Serving Size: Yields twelve skewers.

Ingredients:

- Twenty-four cherry tomatoes
- Twelve little mozzarella sticks
- Twelve new basil leaves
- Balsamic glaze to pour over

Preparation:

1. On each skewer, thread a cherry tomato, a basil leaf, and a little mozzarella ball.
2. Place the skewers in a serving plate arrangement.

3. Serve immediately with a balsamic glaze drizzled over.
4. At room temperature, serve.

Chickpea and Sweet Potato Patties

Description: Taste the earthy deliciousness of sweet potatoes and chickpeas in these nutrient-dense, tasty patties, ideal for a meal that is low in oxalate.

Prep time: 20 minutes

Cooking time: 20 minutes

Ingredients:

- Two medium-sized sweet potatoes, shredded and peeling
- One can (15 oz) of drained and crushed chickpeas
- 1/4 cup of coarsely chopped red onion
- two minced garlic cloves
- Two teaspoons of freshly cut cilantro
- One teaspoon of cumin powder
- One-half tsp paprika
- Add pepper and salt to taste.
- Olive oil for culinary use

Preparation:

1. Grated sweet potatoes, mashed chickpeas, minced garlic, chopped red onion, cilantro, cumin, paprika, salt, and pepper should all be combined in a big bowl.
2. Create patties out of the mixture.
3. Cook the patties until golden brown, about 4–5 minutes per side.
4. Warm up and serve.

Cups of mango and shrimp ceviche

Description: These light and delightful mango and shrimp ceviche cups will raise your beginning game—each mouthful delivers a rush of tropical flavors.

Prep Time: 30 minutes

Serving Size: Yields fifteen cups.

Ingredients:

- One pound of chopped and cooked shrimp
- Dice 2 ripe mangoes; finely cut 1/2 red onion;
- finely chop 1/4 cup fresh cilantro;
- finely chop 1 jalapeño (seed removed);
- And dice 1 avocado.
- quarter-cup lime juice
- Add pepper and salt to taste.
- Serving cups made of tortillas

Preparation:

1. Diced shrimp, mangos, avocado, lime juice, cilantro, jalapeño, red onion, and salt and pepper should all be combined in a dish.
2. Let the flavors settle in by refrigerating for at least an hour.
3. Before serving, spoon ceviche into tortilla cups.
4. Present cold.

Tzatziki Sauced Greek Salad Skewers

Taste the bright tastes of a Greek salad on skewers paired with a cool tzatziki sauce. This is a classy and low-oxalate appetizer that goes well with any meal.

Prep Time: 20 minutes

Serving Size: Yields sixteen skewers.

Ingredients:

- Cut one cucumber into cubes.
- One pint of cherries
- one cup olives, Kalamata
- One cup cubed feta cheese, one-fourth cup finely chopped red onion, and tzatziki sauce for dipping

Preparation:

1. On each skewer, thread a cube of cucumber, a cherry tomato, an olive, a cube of feta, and a sprinkling of red onion.
2. Place the skewers in a serving plate arrangement.
3. Provide tzatziki sauce on the side for dipping.
4. Savor this tasty and refreshing appetizer.
5. These low-oxalate appetizers provide a range of tastes and textures, making them a great way to start any dinner or get-together.

Dressings that Enhance Flavor without Compromising Health

Zesty Lemon Herb Vinaigrette

Description: This light, zesty dressing with a variety of herbs and a blast of citrus lifts salads.

Prep Time: Five minutes

1 Serving

Ingredients:

- 1/4 cup lemon juice, straight
- 1/3 cup of pure olive oil
- 1 tspn of mustard Dijon
- one minced garlic clove
- One tablespoon of freshly chopped parsley
- Add pepper and salt to taste.

Preparation:

1. Lemon juice, olive oil, Dijon mustard, minced garlic, and chopped parsley should all be combined in a bowl.
2. Add pepper and salt to taste.
3. Pour over your preferred salad and mix thoroughly.

Dressing with Dill and Greek Yogurt

Description: A creamy, low-fat dressing that tastes great on salads or as a dip, made with Greek yogurt and fresh dill.

Prep Time: Seven minutes

1 Serving

Ingredients:

- half a cup of yogurt
- Two teaspoons of freshly chopped dill
- One-third cup lemon juice
- One tsp honey
- Add pepper and salt to taste.

Preparation:

1. Greek yogurt, honey, lemon juice, and chopped dill should all be combined in a dish.
2. Mix thoroughly with a whisk.
3. Add pepper and salt to taste.

Maple Balsamic Dijon Dressing

Description: A tart and sweet dressing that counterbalances the sweetness of maple and the sharpness of Dijon with the richness of balsamic.

Prep Time: Five minutes

1 Serving

Ingredients:

- Balsamic vinegar, 1/4 cup
- One-fourth cup of extra virgin olive oil
- Two tsp pure maple syrup
- One spoonful of mustard Dijon
- one minced garlic clove

- Add pepper and salt to taste.

Preparation:

1. Combine the olive oil, maple syrup, Dijon mustard, minced garlic, and balsamic vinegar in a bowl.
2. Use as a marinade for grilled vegetables or drizzle over salads.

Avocado Lime Cilantro Dressing

Description: A colorful and nutrient-dense dressing is made with creamy avocado, zesty lime, and fresh cilantro

Prep time: Seven minutes

Serving Size: around one cup

Ingredients:

- One mature avocado, seeded and sliced
- Lime juice from two
- 1/4 cup finely chopped fresh cilantro
- Half a cup of Greek yogurt
- One spoonful of honey
- Add pepper and salt to taste.

Preparation:

1. Blend together the chopped cilantro, lime juice, Greek yogurt, honey, and peeled avocado in a blender.
2. Mix until homogeneous.
3. Add pepper and salt to taste.

4. Use as a vegetable dip or salad dressing.

Turmeric Tahini Dressing

Description: This golden-hued dressing combines the nutty taste of tahini with the anti-inflammatory properties of turmeric.

Prep Time: Five minutes

Serving Measurements: around 3/4 cup

Ingredients:

- Half a cup tahini
- two tsp of lemon juice
- One tsp of olive oil
- one tsp finely ground turmeric
- One tsp honey
- one minced garlic clove
- Add pepper and salt to taste.

Preparation:

1. Mix the tahini, lemon juice, olive oil, honey, ground turmeric, and chopped garlic in a bowl.
2. Add pepper and salt to taste.
3. Use as a dressing for grain bowls or as a drizzle over roasted veggies.

Raspberry Walnut Vinaigrette

Description: This vinaigrette blends the crunch of walnuts with the acidity of raspberries, creating a sweet and nutty combination.

Prep Time: Five minutes

1 Serving

Ingredients:

- Half a cup raspberries, frozen or fresh
- Two teaspoons of red wine vinegar and 1/4 cup of walnut oil
- One spoonful of honey
- 1/4 cup chopped walnuts
- Add pepper and salt to taste.

Preparation:

1. Puree the raspberries, walnut oil, red wine vinegar, and honey in a blender until the mixture is smooth.
2. Add the chopped walnuts and stir.
3. Add pepper and salt to taste.
4. Use as a vinaigrette for fruit salads or drizzle over mixed greens.

Cilantro Lime Yogurt Dressing

Description: An intensely flavorful and velvety dressing bursting with the vibrancy of lime and the crispness of cilantro, ideal for a flavorful boost to tacos or salads.

1 Serving

Ingredients:

- half a cup of yogurt
- Lime juice from two
- 1/4 cup finely chopped fresh cilantro
- One tsp of olive oil
- one minced garlic clove
- Add pepper and salt to taste.

Preparation:

1. Combine Greek yogurt, olive oil, minced garlic, chopped cilantro, and lime juice in a bowl.
2. Add pepper and salt to taste.
3. Use as a sauce for grilled chicken or as a dressing for taco salads.

Miso Ginger Sesame Dressing

Description: A rich, umami-filled dressing that combines the nutty taste of sesame, the zing of ginger, and the depth of miso.

Prep Time: 8 minutes

3/4 cup Serving

Ingredients:

- Three tsp white miso paste
- Twice as much rice vinegar

- One-third cup soy sauce
- One tsp of sesame oil
- One tablespoon of freshly grated ginger
- One spoonful of honey
- two tsp of water

Preparation:

1. White miso paste, rice vinegar, soy sauce, sesame oil, grated ginger, honey, and water should all be combined in a bowl.
2. If necessary, add additional water to adjust consistency.
3. Pour over Asian-style salads or use as a marinade for chicken or tofu.

A Balsamic Reduction with Orange Basil

Description: This sweet and fragrant reduction mixes the freshness of basil, the richness of balsamic vinegar, and the zesty notes of orange.

Prep Time: 10 minutes

Cooking time: 15 Minutes

Serving: half a cup

Ingredients:

- An orange juice cup
- Balsamic vinegar, half a cup
- two teaspoons finely chopped fresh basil
- One spoonful of honey

Preparation:

1. Orange juice, honey, balsamic vinegar, and chopped basil should all be combined in a pot.
2. Heat to a simmer on a medium setting.
3. After reducing the heat, simmer the mixture for approximately 15 minutes, or until it has thickened.
4. Let cool before sprinkling over grilled veggies or salads.

Hot Cashew Lime Cilantro Cream

Description: Infused with strong tastes of lime and cilantro, this spicy cashew cream dressing is dairy-free and adds a creamy touch to your favorite recipes.

Prep time: Ten minutes

Serving: one cup

Ingredients:

- One cup of uncooked cashews, soaking for one hour in hot water
- 1/4 cup of water
- Lime juice from two
- 1/4 cup chopped fresh cilantro and 1 tsp chili powder
- Add salt to taste.

Preparation:

1. Once soaked, drain and rinse cashews.
2. Cashews, water, lime juice, chopped cilantro, chili powder, and salt should all be combined in a blender.
3. Blend till creamy and smooth.

4. If necessary, add additional water to adjust consistency.
5. Use as a dip for vegetable sticks or as a drizzle over tacos and bowls.

Savory Bites for Social Gatherings

Spinach and Feta Phyllo Triangles

Description: A visually appealing and savory appetizer for any social occasion, these phyllo triangles are loaded with a delicious blend of spinach and feta.

Prep time: 30 minutes

Cooking time: 20 minutes

Ingredients:

- One container (16 ounces) of thawed and drained frozen chopped spinach
- One cup of feta cheese, crumbled
- Half a cup of ricotta
- 1/4 cup of Parmesan cheese, grated
- 1/4 cup of red onion, chopped finely
- two minced garlic cloves
- Add pepper and salt to taste.
- One box of thawed phyllo dough
- Half a cup of melted unsalted butter

Preparation:

1. Turn the oven on to 375°F, or 190°C.

2. The drained spinach, feta, ricotta, Parmesan, red onion, garlic, salt, and pepper should all be combined in a bowl.
3. First, lay down a layer of phyllo dough, then top it with another sheet after brushing it with melted butter. Trim to 3-inch lengths.
4. At one end of each strip, place a dollop of the spinach mixture, then fold into triangles. Continue with the remaining filling and dough.
5. Place the triangles in an arrangement on a baking sheet, and bake for 18 to 20 minutes, or until they are golden brown.

Goat cheese and mushroom crostini

Description: A classy complement to your social event, these bite-sized treats are a lovely combination of creamy goat cheese and earthy mushrooms on crisp crostini.

Prep time: 15 minutes

Cooking time: 10 minutes

Size of Serving: 20 Crostini

Ingredients:

- One sliced French baguette
- Two tsp of olive oil
- Two cups of finely chopped mixed mushrooms
- two minced garlic cloves
- One teaspoon of newly plucked thyme
- Add pepper and salt to taste.
- One cup softened goat cheese

- Garnish with fresh chives.

Preparation:

1. Set oven temperature to 400°F, or 200°C.
2. Place the bread pieces in a single layer on a baking pan, drizzle with olive oil, and cook until they turn golden brown.
3. Add the mushrooms, garlic, and thyme to a pan and cook over medium heat until the mushrooms become brown. Add pepper and salt for seasoning.
4. Cover each crostini with a layer of goat cheese, then top with the mushroom mixture.
5. Serve with fresh chives as a garnish.

Jalapeño Poppers Wrapped in Bacon

Description: These mouthwatering morsels, packed with cream cheese and encased in crispy bacon, are sure to be a favorite at any get-together.

Prep time: Twenty minutes

Cooking time: twenty-five minutes for cooking

Size of Serving: 16 Poppers

Ingredients:

- Eight huge jalapeños, seeded and half
- 8 ounces of softened cream cheese
- One cup of cheddar cheese, shredded
- Cut eight bacon strips in half.
- Toothpaste

Preparation:

1. Before proceeding, preheat the oven to 375°F (190°C) and place parchment paper on a baking pan.
2. Combine the shredded cheddar and softened cream cheese in a bowl and stir until thoroughly blended.
3. Divide the cream cheese mixture between each side of a jalapeño.
4. Put a half-slice of bacon around each packed jalapeño and fasten it with toothpicks.
5. Put on the baking pan and bake until the bacon crisps, about 25 minutes.

Skewers of caprese with a balsamic glaze

Description: These skewers of Caprese, a classic with a modern twist, are ideal as a light and refreshing appetizer since they contain fresh mozzarella, cherry tomatoes, and basil drizzled with a balsamic glaze.

Prep time: 15 minutes

Size of Serving: 24 Skewers

Ingredients:

- Twenty-four new mozzarella balls
- Twenty-four cherry tomatoes
- fresh leaves of basil
- Balsamic glaze to drizzle over skewers of wood

Preparation:

1. On each skewer, thread one mozzarella ball, one cherry tomato, and one basil leaf.
2. Place the skewers in a serving plate arrangement.
3. Before serving, pour some balsamic glaze over the dish.

Gruyère and Caramelized Onion Tartlets

Description: These sophisticated tartlets have a buttery pastry shell that encases the rich taste of Gruyère cheese and the sweetness of caramelized onions.

Prep time: 30 minutes

Cooking time: 25 minutes

Serving Size: Eighteen Pies

Ingredients:

- Two tsp of olive oil
- Two big onions, cut thinly
- One tsp sugar
- One sheet of thawed puff pastry and one cup of grated Gruyère cheese
- Fresh leaves of thyme for decoration

Preparation:

1. Using the pan Heat the olive oil over medium heat
2. Add the sugar and the sliced onions, and cook for 15 to 20 minutes, or until the onions are caramelized.
3. Warm up the oven to 400°F, or 200°C, and coat small tart pans with oil.

4. To fit the tartlet pans, roll out the puff pastry and cut into rounds. In the pans, press the pastry.
5. Fill each tartlet shell with caramelized onions, then garnish with grated Gruyère.
6. Bake for twenty-five minutes, or until the cheese has melted and the crust is brown.
7. Before serving, garnish with fresh thyme leaves.

Smoked Salmon and Cream Cheese Cucumber Bites

Description: These cool cucumber bits with a herbed cream cheese and smoked salmon on top provide a flavor explosion that is ideal for any get-together.

Prep time: 20 minutes

Serving Quantity: 20 pieces

Ingredients:

- One English cucumber, sliced; eight ounces of melted cream cheese
- One tablespoon capers and two teaspoons of freshly chopped dill
- 4 ounces of strip-cut smoked salmon
- slices of lemon as a garnish

Preparation:

1. Combine chopped fresh dill with melted cream cheese in a bowl.
2. Arrange the cucumber slices on a dish for serving.
3. Top each piece of cucumber with a dab of herbed cream cheese.

4. Add some capers and a piece of smoked salmon on top.
5. Before serving, garnish with lemon wedges.

Hot and Spicy Chicken Satay Sticks

Description: For those who love spicy and robust appetizers, these skewers with tender chicken marinated in a fiery combination of Asian-inspired spices will thrill.

Prep time: 30 minutes

Cooking time: 15 minutes

Size of Serving: 20 Skewers

Ingredients:

- 1.5 pounds of skinless, boneless, and sliced chicken thighs
- 1/4 cup sesame oil
- Twice as much peanut butter
- Two tsp of honey
- One spoonful of hot sauce
- two minced garlic cloves
- 1 tsp finely chopped ginger
- Water-soaked wooden skewers

Preparation:

1. To create the marinade, combine the soy sauce, grated ginger, honey, peanut butter, and Sriracha in a bowl.
2. After skewering the chicken strips, soak them and arrange them in a shallow plate.

3. After covering the chicken skewers with marinade, let them sit for at least 20 minutes.
4. Turn the heat up to medium-high on the grill or grill pan.
5. Turn the skewers once or twice while grilling them for about 6 to 8 minutes, or until the chicken is well cooked.

Herb Cream Cheese Stuffed Mushrooms with Garlic

Description: These stuffed mushrooms are the ideal snack for any social gathering, with a savory blend of garlic and herb cream cheese within. They are a bite-sized blast of flavor.

Prep time: Twenty minutes

Cooking time: twenty minutes

Quantity served: 24 mushrooms

Ingredients:

- 24 big white mushrooms with their stems cut off and set aside
- 8 ounces of softened cream cheese
- two minced garlic cloves
- Two teaspoons of freshly chopped parsley
- Add pepper and salt to taste.
- half a cup of crumbs
- Two tsp finely shredded Parmesan cheese

Preparation:

1. Turn the oven on to 375°F (190°C) and coat a baking dish with oil.
2. Chop the saved stems of the mushrooms finely.
3. Combine cream cheese, chopped parsley, minced garlic, salt, and pepper in a bowl.
4. Mix well after adding the breadcrumbs and chopped mushroom stems.
5. After stuffing the cream cheese mixture into each mushroom cap, put them on the baking dish.
6. After adding some Parmesan cheese, roast the mushrooms for 20 minutes, or until they are soft.

Tiny Pizzas Margherita

Description: These bite-sized Margherita pizzas are a popular and delicious option for any social event. They have fresh tomatoes, mozzarella, and basil on a crispy crust.

Prep time: 25 minutes

Cooking time: 15 minutes

Size of Serving: 24 Mini Pizzas

Ingredients:

- Two pieces of pizza dough from the store
- a single cup of sauce
- Two cups of freshly sliced mozzarella
- Two cups of halved cherry tomatoes
- For garnish, use fresh basil leaves.
- Use olive oil to drizzle

Preparation:

1. Adjust the oven temperature to 425°F (220°C) and place parchment paper on a baking pan.
2. Using a round cutter, roll out the pizza dough and cut off little pizza rounds.
3. Spread tomato sauce over each of the little pizza circles that you have placed on the baking sheet.
4. Garnish with cherry tomato halves and sliced mozzarella.
5. Bake for 12 to 15 minutes, or until the cheese melts and the crust turns brown.
6. Before serving, sprinkle some fresh basil leaves on top and pour some olive oil over it.

Cups of Black Bean and Avocado Salsa

Description: A vivid and refreshing complement to your social event, these vibrant salsa cups blend the fiery black bean salsa with the creamy deliciousness of avocados, all presented in crispy tortilla cups.

Cooking/Prep Time: 10 minutes for baking, 20 minutes for prep

20 salsa cups are served.

Ingredients:

- Ten little flour tortillas
- One cup of rinsed and drained black beans; two ripe avocados, chopped
- One cup of frozen or fresh corn kernels
- one cup of chopped cherry tomatoes
- 1/4 cup of coarsely chopped red onion
- 1/4 cup finely chopped cilantro
- Lime juice from two

- Add pepper and salt to taste.

Preparation:

1. Turn the oven on to 375°F, or 190°C.
2. Each tortilla should be cut into quarters, which should then be pressed into a tiny muffin tray to create cups.
3. Bake the tortilla cups for 8 to 10 minutes, or until they are crisp and golden.
4. Diced avocados, black beans, corn, cherry tomatoes, red onion, cilantro, lime juice, salt, and pepper should all be combined in a bowl.
5. Before serving, spoon the black bean salsa and avocado into the baked tortilla cups.

Quick and Nutrient-Rich Appetizers

Mango Avocado Salsa Cups

Description: This nutrient-dense, delicious appetizer combines the sweetness of mango with the creamy texture of avocado to create a blast of tropical tastes with each bite.

Prep time: 15 minutes

Portion Size: 16 ounces

Ingredients:

- Two ripe mangos, two sliced avocados, half a diced red onion, 1/4 cup finely chopped fresh cilantro,
- Lime juice from two
- Add pepper and salt to taste.

- sixteen little tortilla cups

Preparation:

1. Diced mangos, avocados, red onion, cilantro, lime juice, salt, and pepper should all be combined in a dish.
2. Fill the tortilla cups with the mango-avocado mixture using a spoon.
3. If desired, add more cilantro as a garnish.
4. Serve right away and savor!

Platter of Greek Yogurt Vegetable Dip

Description: A healthful and gratifying snack for any occasion, this fast and nutrient-rich dip combines Greek yogurt with a mix of vibrant vegetables.

Prep time: Ten minutes

Serving Size: Eight Dips

Ingredients:

- Greek yogurt, one cup
- half a cup of coarsely chopped cucumber
- quartered cherry tomatoes, half a cup
- 1/4 cup finely chopped red bell pepper 1/4 cup sliced green onions 1 tablespoon finely chopped fresh dill
- Add pepper and salt to taste.
- Various fresh vegetables to dip

Preparation:

1. Greek yogurt, cucumber, cherry tomatoes, red bell pepper, green onions, and fresh dill should all be combined in a dish.
2. Add pepper and salt to taste.
3. Place a dish with the dip in the middle and a variety of fresh vegetables around it.
4. Serve as a vibrant and wholesome dip plate.

Pita Chips paired with Edamame Hummus

Description: Improve your hummus game with this variation that includes edamame. Serve it with freshly cooked pita chips for a delightful and healthful snack that's loaded with nutrients.

Cooking/Prep Time: 10 minutes for baking, 15 minutes for prep

8 Serving

Ingredients:

- Two cups of prepared edamame
- Half a cup tahini
- two minced garlic cloves
- lime juice from one
- Two tsp of olive oil
- Add pepper and salt to taste.
- Cut the pita bread into triangles.

Preparation:

1. Process the edamame, tahini, lemon juice, olive oil, minced garlic, salt, and pepper in a food processor until smooth.
2. Taste and adjust the seasoning.

3. To make pita chips, place triangles on a baking sheet, drizzle with a little olive oil, and bake for 8 to 10 minutes, or until crisp and golden.
4. Serve the handmade pita chips alongside the edamame hummus.

Mini Bell Peppers Stuffed

Description: These little stuffed peppers are a colorful and nutrient-dense garnish for any appetizer presentation. They are loaded with a flavorful blend of black beans, veggies, and quinoa.

Cooking/Prep Time: 20 minutes cook time, 15 minutes bake time

Ingredients:

- Ten small bell peppers, cut in half and without seeds
- 1 cup of quinoa, cooked
- Half a cup of rinsed and drained black beans
- 1/4 cup kernels of corn
- 1/4 cup chopped cherry tomatoes
- 1/4 cup of coarsely chopped red onion
- 1/4 cup of cheddar cheese, shredded
- fresh cilantro to decorate

Preparation:

1. Turn the oven on to 375°F, or 190°C.
2. Combine the cooked quinoa, corn, black beans, red onion, cherry tomatoes, and shredded cheddar cheese in a bowl.
3. Place a spoonful of the mixture into each small bell pepper half.

4. Bake peppers for 15 minutes, or until soft.
5. Before serving, garnish with fresh cilantro.

Roll-Ups with Cucumber and Hummus

Description: These crisp and crispy cucumber roll-ups, stuffed with smooth hummus, are a healthy and nutritious snack that's simple to prepare and devour.

Prep time: 15 minutes

Size of Serving: 16 Roll-ups

Ingredients:

- Two big cucumbers
- Cup of hummus
- Sliced cherry tomatoes (for garnish)
- Chopped fresh parsley (for garnish)

Preparation:

1. Cut the cucumbers into thin lengthwise slices using a vegetable peeler.
2. Drizzle each slice of cucumber with a little amount of hummus.
3. Slices of cucumber should be rolled up and fastened with toothpicks.
4. Add chopped fresh parsley and cherry tomato slices as garnish.
5. Place on a serving dish and savor this crisp and light snack.

Asparagus Bundles Wrapped in Prosciutto

Description: Prosciutto-wrapped asparagus bundles are a classy appetizer perfect for any occasion. They are tasty and elegant, with a lovely blend of crisp asparagus and savory prosciutto.

Cooking/Prep Time: 15 minutes bake, 15 minutes prep

16 Serving

Ingredients:

- 32 asparagus spears, thinned 8 prosciutto slices, sliced lengthwise in half
- Use olive oil to drizzle
- Balsamic glaze to pour over

Preparation:

1. Adjust the oven temperature to 400°F (200°C) and place parchment paper on a baking pan.
2. Twist two asparagus stalks together, then enclose with a prosciutto half.
3. After placing the bundles on the baking sheet and brushing them with olive oil, bake for fifteen minutes, or until the prosciutto is crisp and the asparagus is soft.
4. Before serving, drizzle with balsamic glaze.

Stuffed Avocado Halves with Quinoa Salad

Description: Packed with nutrition and protein, these avocado halves filled with quinoa salad make a healthy, visually beautiful, and incredibly tasty appetizer.

Prep time: 20 minutes

8 Serving

Ingredients:

- 1 cup of quinoa, cooked
- Half a cup of cherry tomatoes
- half a cup of chopped cucumber
- 1/4 cup of coarsely chopped red onion
- 1/4 cup of crumbled feta cheese
- Two teaspoons of freshly chopped parsley
- lime juice from one
- Add pepper and salt to taste.
- Four avocados, pitted and halved

Preparation:

1. Cooked quinoa, cherry tomatoes, cucumber, red onion, feta cheese, parsley, lemon juice, salt, and pepper should all be combined in a bowl.
2. Fill the half avocados with the quinoa salad.
3. Serve right away for a filling and nutrient-dense appetizer.

Chickpea and Sweet Potato Bites

Description: The combination of perfectly seasoned roasted sweet potatoes and chickpeas creates these delectable nibbles, which make for a pleasant, nutrient-rich, and substantial appetizer.

Cooking/Prep Time: 20 minutes for preparation and 25 minutes for baking

Serving Quantity: 24 pieces

Ingredients:

- Two medium-sized sweet potatoes, chopped and skinned
- One can (15 oz) of rinsed and drained chickpeas
- Two tsp of olive oil
- One tsp cumin
- One tsp of paprika
- One-half tsp of garlic powder
- Add salt and pepper to suit. You can also add Greek yogurt for dipping.

Preparation:

1. Adjust the oven temperature to 400°F (200°C) and place parchment paper on a baking pan.
2. Diced sweet potatoes and chickpeas should be combined with olive oil, salt, pepper, paprika, cumin, and garlic powder in a bowl.
3. After spreading the mixture onto the baking sheet, bake the sweet potatoes for 25 minutes, or until they are soft.
4. If preferred, serve the chickpea and sweet potato bits with Greek yogurt for dipping.

Basil Tomato Bruschetta

Description: A traditional bruschetta that combines the tastes of fresh basil, juicy tomatoes, and balsamic sauce in a light and nutritious snack that is sure to satisfy any crowd.

Cooking/Prep Time: 10 minutes for broiling and 15 minutes for prep

16-slice serving size

Ingredients:

- 4 big tomatoes, minced garlic cloves, chopped 1/2 cup fresh basil, and 2 tablespoons balsamic glaze
- Garlic powder and salt to taste Baguette, cut

Preparation:

1. Diced tomatoes, minced garlic, basil, balsamic glaze, salt, and pepper should all be combined in a bowl.
2. Place the baguette pieces on a baking pan and toast them gently under the broiler for two to three minutes.
3. Place a spoonful of the tomato basil mixture on each piece of toasted baguette.
4. Serve right away for a tasty and easy appetizer.

Veggie Dippers with Beet Hummus

Description: Bright and full of nutrients, this beet hummus gives a traditional dip a vibrant new look. It is a healthy and convenient appetizer when served with a variety of vegetable dippers.

Prep time: 15 minutes

Serving Size: Ten Dips

Ingredients:

- One can (15 oz) of rinsed and drained chickpeas
- two cooked and peeled medium-sized beets
- Half a cup tahini
- two minced garlic cloves
- lime juice from one

- Two tsp of olive oil
- Add pepper and salt to taste.
- a variety of veggie sticks to dip

Preparation:

1. Puree the chickpeas, cooked beets, tahini, lemon juice, olive oil, minced garlic, salt, and pepper in a food processor until smooth.
2. Taste and adjust the seasoning.
3. Serve the bright and nutrient-dense beet hummus with a variety of veggie sticks.

Chapter 3: Satisfying Soups and Salads:

Nourishing Broths and Soups

Traditional Soup with Noodles

Description: A filling bowl that calms the spirit, this chicken noodle soup is a soothing and ageless classic. It's loaded with succulent chicken, substantial veggies, and mouthwatering noodles.

Prep time: 20 minutes

Cooking time: 30 minutes

6 Servings

Ingredients:

- 1 pound of cooked, shredded, skinless, boneless chicken breasts
- Eight cups chicken stock
- Two carrots, cut into slices; two celery stalks; one onion, chopped; two minced garlic cloves
- two cups of ramen
- A single tsp of dried thyme
- Add pepper and salt to taste.
- For garnish, use fresh parsley.

Preparation:

1. Add the garlic and onions to a large saucepan and sauté until softened.

2. Stir in the carrots, celery, thyme, chicken broth, salt, and pepper. Heat till boiling.
3. Once the noodles are soft, reduce heat, add the shredded chicken and egg noodles, and simmer.
4. Before serving, add some fresh parsley as a garnish and adjust the spice as necessary.

Vegetarian Lentil Soup

Description: A satisfying bowl of plant-based delight, this vegetarian lentil soup is full of fiber and protein and has a variety of vibrant veggies and flavorful spices.

Prep time: 15 minutes

Cooking time: 40 minutes

8 Serving

Ingredients:

- One cup washed and dried green lentils,
- eight cups vegetable broth,
- two chopped carrots,
- two diced celery stalks, one diced onion,
- three diced cloves of garlic, minced garlic,
- and one can (14 oz) cut-up tomatoes
- One teaspoon of cumin powder
- One tsp finely ground coriander
- One-half tsp smoked paprika
- Add pepper and salt to taste.
- fresh cilantro to decorate

Preparation:

1. Fry the garlic and onions in a big saucepan until aromatic.
2. Lentils, carrots, celery, chopped tomatoes, smoked paprika, cumin, and coriander should all be added along with salt and pepper. Heat till boiling.
3. Lentils should be tender after 30 to 40 minutes of simmering over low heat.
4. Before serving, garnish with fresh cilantro.

Soup with Creamy Tomato Basil

Description: Savor the velvety richness of this creamy tomato basil soup, which is the ideal combination of juicy tomatoes, fragrant basil, and a hint of cream. It's a filling dish that exudes elegance and coziness.

Prep time: 15 minutes

Cooking time: 30 minutes

6 Servings

Ingredients:

- One 28-oz can of crushed tomatoes
- 4 cups vegetable broth; 1 chopped onion
- three minced garlic cloves, half a cup of fresh basil leaves, one cup of heavy cream
- Add pepper and salt to taste.
- Parmesan cheese, grated, as a garnish

Preparation:

1. Sauté garlic and onions in a saucepan until they become tender.
2. Add chopped basil, vegetable broth, and smashed tomatoes. Simmer for a while.
3. Using an immersion blender, puree the soup until it's completely smooth.
4. After adding the heavy cream and seasoning with salt and pepper, simmer for a further ten minutes.
5. Top with some grated Parmesan cheese before serving.

Tom Kha Gai, a spicy Thai coconut soup

Description: Take a taste adventure with Tom Kha Gai, a spicy Thai coconut soup. It's a flavorful concoction of lemongrass, chili, and coconut milk with soft chicken and bright veggies.

Prep time: Twenty minutes

Cooking time: twenty-five minutes

4 Servings

Ingredients:

- 1 pound of sliced, skinless, boneless chicken thighs and 4 cups of chicken broth
- One 14-oz can of coconut milk
- Two stalks of lemongrass, three smashed kaffir lime leaves, one sliced red bell pepper, one cup of sliced mushrooms, and two teaspoons of fish sauce
- One-third cup soy sauce
- One-third cup lime juice
- One-third cup brown sugar
- Two sliced red chilies (optional)

- fresh cilantro to decorate

Preparation:

1. Heat coconut milk, lemongrass, kaffir lime leaves, and chicken broth in a saucepan until they start to gently boil.
2. Add the bell pepper, mushrooms, fish sauce, soy sauce, brown sugar, lime juice, and sliced chicken. Cook the chicken by simmering it.
3. Take out the kaffir lime leaves and lemongrass. For further spiciness, adjust the seasoning and add chopped chilies.
4. Before serving, garnish with fresh cilantro.

Filling Minestrone Soup

Description: This powerful minestrone soup, which combines pasta, beans, and veggies, is a filling and nutritious dish that perfectly embodies Italian comfort food.

Prep time: 20 minutes

Cooking time: 40 minutes

8 Serving

Ingredients:

- Two tsp of olive oil
- Chop one onion.
- Three garlic cloves, two carrots chopped, two celery stalks diced, one zucchini diced, and one can (14 oz) diced cut-up tomatoes
- One can (15 oz) of washed and drained cannellini beans

- Six cups of vegetable stock
- One cup of tiny pasta, such as ditalini
- One tsp of dehydrated oregano
- One tsp of dehydrated basil
- Add pepper and salt to taste.
- Parmesan cheese, grated, as a garnish

Preparation:

1. Add the garlic and onions to a large saucepan and sauté in olive oil until tender.
2. Add the chopped tomatoes, zucchini, carrots, celery, cannellini beans, vegetable broth, basil, oregano, and salt and pepper. Heat till boiling.
3. Once the pasta is done, reduce heat and simmer.
4. After adjusting the spice, top the dish with a little grated Parmesan cheese.

Ginger Carrot Soup with Turmeric

Description: Savor the therapeutic qualities of ginger and turmeric in this colorful soup of carrots. It's a tasty, silky bowl of sustenance that lifts the soul and body.

Prep time: 15 minutes

Cooking time: 25 minutes

6 Servings

Ingredients:

- Two tsp of coconut oil
- Chop one onion.
- three minced garlic cloves

- One pound of peeled and sliced carrots
- One tablespoon of freshly grated ginger
- one tsp finely ground turmeric
- Four cups of vegetable stock
- 14 oz. (one can) milk from coconuts
- Add pepper and salt to taste.
- fresh cilantro to decorate

Preparation:

1. Add the garlic and onions to a saucepan and cook over medium heat until fragrant.
2. Stir in the ground turmeric, grated ginger, sliced carrots, vegetable broth, and coconut milk.
3. Simmer for a while.
4. Cook carrots until they become soft.
5. **Using an immersion blender, puree the soup until it's completely smooth.**
6. Before serving, add a dash of fresh cilantro and season with salt and pepper.

Miso Udon Soup with Vegetables and Tofu

Description: This bowl of nutritious Miso Udon Soup fills the palette and the spirit with its comfortable combination of chewy udon noodles, umami-rich miso, tofu, and various veggies.

Prep Time: 15 minutes

Cooking time: 20 minutes

Ingredients:

- Udon noodles, 8 oz.
- Four cups of vegetable stock
- Two teaspoons of miso paste (white)
- One cup cubed firm tofu, one cup sliced shiitake mushrooms, one cup chopped baby bok choy, two sliced green onions, and one tablespoon soy sauce
- One tsp of sesame oil
- Sunflower seeds as a garnish

Preparation:

1. Udon noodles should be prepared as directed on the package and then placed aside.
2. Simmer the veggie stock in a saucepan. Add miso paste and whisk until dissolved.
3. Add the baby bok choy, sesame oil, shiitake mushrooms, green onions, and tofu.
4. 4. Cook the vegetables until they are tender.
5. Spoon cooked udon noodles into bowls, then cover with miso broth.
6. Serve with sesame seeds as a garnish.

Roasted Butternut Squash Soup

Description: A rich and filling option for chilly days, this soup has a silky combination of roasted butternut squash, fragrant spices, and a hint of cream.

Cooking/Prep Time: 40 minutes for baking, 20 minutes for prep

6 Servings

Ingredients:

- One big butternut squash, chopped and skinned
- Two tsp of olive oil
- Four cups of veggie broth and one teaspoon of ground cinnamon
- One-half tsp ground nutmeg
- Half a cup of heavy cream
- Add pepper and salt to taste.
- Cantaloupe seeds as garnish

Preparation:

1. Add olive oil and toss with cubed butternut squash, onions, and garlic. Roast the squash at 400°F, or 200°C, in the oven until it is soft.
2. Blend the roasted vegetables and vegetable broth in a blender until the mixture is smooth.
3. After transferring the purée to a saucepan, mix in the hcavy cream, nutmeg, cinnamon, and pepper. Simmer until well heated.
4. Before serving, sprinkle some pumpkin seeds on top.

Lemon Chicken Orzo Soup

Description: A healthy bowl that brightens any day, this soup combines soft orzo, juicy chicken, and a zesty touch to create a refreshing take on a classic. Orzo soup with lemon chicken.

Prep Time: 15 minutes

Cooking time: 30 minutes

6 Servings

Ingredients:

- One pound of cooked and shredded chicken thighs without any bones or skin
- Eight cups chicken stock
- one cup pasta, orzo
- cut into two pieces
- two chopped celery stalks
- Chop one onion.
- three minced garlic cloves
- Juice and zest from two lemons
- A single tsp of dried thyme
- Add pepper and salt to taste.
- Garnish with fresh dill

Preparation:

1. Add the garlic and onions to a large saucepan and sauté until softened.
2. Add the orzo, carrots, celery, thyme, shredded chicken, chicken broth, salt, and pepper. Heat till boiling.
3. Once the veggies are soft and the orzo is done, lower the heat and simmer.
4. Add lemon juice and zest and stir. Taste and adjust seasoning.
5. Before serving, garnish with fresh dill.

Vegetable Curry with Coconut Soup

Description: This is a healthy bowl of fragrant and fulfilling coconut curry vegetable soup. Dive into the unique tastes of this combination of colorful veggies drenched in a thick coconut and curry broth.

Prep time: **20 minutes**

Cooking time: 30 minutes

6 Servings

Ingredients:

- Two tsp of coconut oil
- Chop one onion.

- three minced garlic cloves
- One tablespoon of freshly grated ginger
- Twice as much red curry paste
- Four cups of vegetable stock
- One 14-oz can of coconut milk
- cut into two pieces
- 1 sliced bell pepper
- One chopped zucchini
- one cup florets of broccoli
- 1 cup of leafy spinach
- One-third cup soy sauce
- 1 lime's juice
- fresh cilantro to decorate

Preparation:

1. Ginger, garlic, and onions should be sautéed in coconut oil in a saucepan until aromatic.
2. Stir in red curry paste until well mixed.
3. Pour in coconut milk and vegetable broth. Simmer for a while.
4. Add the bell pepper, zucchini, broccoli, spinach, and carrots.
5. **Cook the vegetables until they are tender.**
6. Add lime juice and soy sauce and stir. Taste and adjust seasoning.
7. Before serving, garnish with fresh cilantro.

With their many tastes and ingredients, these filling soups and broths give coziness and warmth in every bowl. Savor the culinary adventure of creating and eating these tasty, healthful treats!

Creative Low-Oxalate Salad Combinations

Citrus Avocado Salad with Quinoa

Description: This colorful salad is low in oxalate and refreshing because it mixes the creamy texture of avocado with the zesty flavor of oranges and a protein boost from quinoa.

Prep time: 20 minutes

Cooking time: 15 minutes

Ingredients:

- One cup of cooked and cooled quinoa
- Two chopped avocados and two sliced oranges
- 1/4 cup finely chopped red onion;
- 1/4 cup finely chopped fresh cilantro; and 1/4 cup lime juice
- Add pepper and salt to taste.

Preparation:

1. Cooked quinoa, chopped cilantro,
2. sliced avocados, orange segments,
3. And red onion should all be combined in a big bowl.
4. Pour in the lime juice and toss lightly to mix.
5. Add pepper and salt to taste.
6. Serve right away or put in the fridge until you're ready to eat.

Watermelon and Mint Cucumber Salad

Description: This delightful salad with low oxalate content combines luscious watermelon and crisp cucumber, all mixed in a cool mint dressing, is a great way to beat the heat.

Prep time: 15 minutes

6 Servings.

Ingredients:

- One finely sliced cucumber, four cups watermelon, one-fourth cup chopped fresh mint leaves, and two tablespoons crumbled feta cheese
- One tsp of olive oil
- One-third cup balsamic vinegar

- Add pepper and salt to taste.

Preparation:

1. Cucumber slices, cubed watermelon, chopped mint, and crumbled feta should all be combined in a big bowl.
2. In a small bowl, combine the olive oil and balsamic vinegar.
3. After drizzling the salad with the dressing, gently toss to coat.
4. Add pepper and salt to taste.
5. Before serving, let the food cool for at least half an hour in the refrigerator.

Salad with Grilled Zucchini Ribbons

Description: This grilled zucchini ribbon salad, which has tiny zucchini slices, cherry tomatoes, and a lemony vinaigrette, will up your salad game.

Cooking/Prep Time: 10 minutes on the grill and 15 minutes on the prep

Ingredients:

- Three zucchini cut lengthwise into thin slice
- Half a cup of cherry tomatoes
- 1/4 cup roasted pine nuts

- 1/4 cup of shaved Parmesan cheese
- lime juice from one
- Three tsp olive oil

Preparation:

1. Turn the heat up to medium-high in a grill pan.
2. Grill the zucchini slices until grill marks form, one to two minutes each side.
3. Grilled zucchini, cherry tomatoes, toasted pine nuts, and shaved Parmesan should all be combined in a dish.
4. Mix the olive oil and lemon juice in a little basin.
5. Pour the dressing over the salad and give it a little stir.

Goat cheese and strawberry salad with arugula

Description: This delectable low-oxalate salad combines creamy goat cheese, peppery arugula, and juicy strawberries in a balsamic vinaigrette. It's sweet and flavorful.

Prep time: 15 minutes

Ingredients:

- 4 portions arugula

- One cup of hulled and sliced strawberries
- 1/4 cup crumbled goat cheese
- Half a tsp balsamic vinegar
- Three tsp olive oil
- One tsp honey

Preparation:

1. Combine arugula, sliced strawberries, and crumbled goat cheese in a big bowl.
2. Combine the olive oil, honey, balsamic vinegar, salt, and pepper in a small bowl.
3. After drizzling the salad with the dressing, gently toss to coat.
4. For a tasty and light meal, serve right away.

Salad with "Couscous" cauliflower

Description: This dish, a low-carb take on a traditional couscous salad, combines colorful greens, finely chopped cauliflower, and a lemon-herb dressing for a light, oxalate-friendly meal.

Prep time: 20 minutes

Ingredients:

- One medium cauliflower, finely chopped or grated

- One cup of quartered cherry tomatoes and one sliced cucumber
- 1/4 cup chopped Kalamata olives;
- 1/4 cup crumbled feta cheese
- lime juice from one
- Three tsp olive oil
- One tsp of dehydrated oregano

Preparation:

1. Grated cauliflower, cherry tomatoes, chopped cucumber, sliced Kalamata olives, and crumbled feta should all be combined in a big bowl.
2. Combine the lemon juice, olive oil, dried oregano, salt, and pepper in a small bowl.
3. Pour the dressing over the salad and give it a little stir.
4. Before serving, let the food cool for at least half an hour in the refrigerator.

Chickpea and Carrot Salad with Turmeric

Description: This salad of roasted carrots and chickpeas, accentuated with fresh herbs and a lemon-tahini vinaigrette, is a tasty and low-oxalate way to embrace the golden hues of turmeric.

Prep time: 20 minutes

Twenty minutes for roasting

Ingredients:

- Cut four big carrots into rounds after peeling them.
- One can (15 oz) of rinsed and drained chickpeas
- Two tsp of olive oil
- one tsp finely ground turmeric
- One tsp cumin
- Add pepper and salt to taste.
- Chopped fresh parsley (for garnish)
- Lemon-tahini dressing (recipe follows)
- Tahini-Lemon Dressing:
- Triple-spooned tahini
- lime juice from one
- Two tsp of olive oil
- one minced garlic clove
- Add pepper and salt to taste.

Preparation:

1. Adjust the oven temperature to 400°F (200°C) and place parchment paper on a baking pan.
2. Sliced carrots and chickpeas should be combined with olive oil, cumin, ground turmeric, salt, and pepper in a dish.

3. After spreading the mixture onto the baking sheet, roast the carrots for 25 minutes, or until they are soft.
4. To create the dressing, combine the tahini, lemon juice, olive oil, chopped garlic, salt, and pepper in a small bowl.
5. Spread the chickpea and roasted carrot mixture onto a dish, sprinkle with the lemon-tahini dressing, and top with the fresh parsley.

Walnut and Pomegranate Arugula Salad

Description: This colorful salad highlights the richness of arugula by combining crisp walnuts, juicy pomegranate seeds, and a zesty vinaigrette for a surprising combination of flavors and textures.

Prep time: 15 minutes

4 Servings

Ingredients:

- 4 portions arugula
- one cup of seed pomegranates
- chopped walnuts, half a cup
- 1/4 cup of shaved Parmesan cheese
- lime juice from one
- Three tsp olive oil

- 1 tspn of mustard Dijon
- Add pepper and salt to taste.

Preparation:

1. Shaved Parmesan, chopped walnuts, pomegranate seeds, and arugula should all be combined in a big bowl.
2. Combine the lemon juice, olive oil, Dijon mustard, salt, and pepper in a small bowl.
3. After drizzling the salad with the dressing, gently toss to coat.
4. For a tasty and nutrient-rich salad, serve right away.

Bacon and Broccoli Raw Cauliflower Salad

Description: This meal, which is a low-oxalate substitute for classic broccoli salad, combines crunchy bacon, crispy cauliflower rice, and a zesty dressing to create a filling and healthy salad.

Prep Time: 20 minutes

Cooking time: 10 minutes

6 Servings

Ingredients:

- one medium-sized riced cauliflower head
- One cup of chopped broccoli florets and six cooked and crumbled bacon pieces
- Half a cup of finely chopped red onion
- one-half cup mayonnaise
- Half a cup of apple cider vinegar
- One spoonful of mustard Dijon
- One spoonful of honey
- Add pepper and salt to taste.

Preparation:

1. Riced cauliflower, chopped broccoli, crumbled bacon, and chopped red onion should all be combined in a big bowl.
2. Combine mayonnaise, apple cider vinegar, Dijon mustard, honey, salt, and pepper in a small bowl.
3. After adding the dressing to the salad, gently toss to mix.

Almond-topped spinach and blueberry salad

Savor the deliciousness of this spinach and blueberry salad, which is enhanced by the crunchy almonds and the mild balsamic vinaigrette. It is packed with antioxidants.

15 minutes for preparation

4 Serving

Ingredients:

- Six cups baby kale
- One cup of berries
- 1/4 cup feta cheese, 1/2 cup sliced almonds, and crumbled balsamic vinaigrette (recipe is below)
- Balsamic Dressing:
- Three tsp balsamic vinegar
- Two tsp of olive oil
- One tsp honey
- Add pepper and salt to taste.

Preparation:

1. Combine baby spinach, blue cheese, and
2. feta crumbles, toasted sliced almonds, and
3. To make the vinaigrette, combine the olive oil, honey, balsamic vinegar, salt, and pepper in a small bowl.
4. After drizzling the salad with the vinaigrette, gently toss to coat.
5. For a nutrient-rich and refreshing experience, serve right away.

Skewers of caprese salad

Description: These skewers, which combine cherry tomatoes, fresh mozzarella, and basil with a balsamic sauce, are a playful and bite-sized take on the traditional Caprese salad and make a great low-oxalate appetizer.

15 minutes for preparation;

12 skewers.

Ingredients:

- Twenty-four cherry tomatoes
- Twenty-four new mozzarella balls
- 24 new leaves of basil
- Balsamic glaze to pour over
- Water-soaked wooden skewers

Preparation:

1. Put a cherry tomato, a ball of fresh mozzarella, and a leaf of basil on a skewer.
2. Place the skewers in a serving plate arrangement.
3. Drizzle the skewers with balsamic glaze right before serving.
4. Serve these delicious skewers of Caprese salad for a visually pleasing and delicious low-oxalate alternative.

A satisfying and nutrient-rich meal experience is guaranteed by the range of tastes and textures offered by these inventive low-oxalate salad combinations. Savor these salads on their own or as an accompaniment to your main entrée.

Chapter 4: Side Dishes for Wellness:

Wholesome Grain Alternatives

Stuffed peppers with black beans and quinoa

This recipe is a healthy take on stuffed peppers, made with quinoa and black bean filling that results in a filling and tasty meal.

Size of Serving: 4 Peppers

Cooking/Preparation Time: 20 minutes cooking, 30 minutes baking

Ingredients:

- One cup of cooked quinoa
- One can (15 oz) of rinsed and drained black beans
- One cup of kernel corn
- 1 cup of tomatoes, diced
- One cup of cheddar cheese, shredded
- 4 bell peppers, cut in half, and seeds taken out
- Season tacos to taste
- fresh cilantro to decorate

Preparation:

1. Set oven temperature to 375°F, or 190°C.
2. Combine the cooked quinoa, diced tomatoes, black beans, corn, shredded cheddar, and taco seasoning in a bowl.
3. Stuff the quinoa mixture into each side of a bell pepper.

4. After placing the filled peppers on a baking tray, bake them for 20 minutes while covered with foil. After removing the foil, roast the peppers for a further 10 minutes, or until they are soft.
5. Add some fresh cilantro as a garnish and serve.

Stir-fried brown rice with vegetables

Description: A tasty and speedy stir-fry with a vibrant array of veggies and brown rice. This hearty recipe is ideal for a nourishing evening supper.

Prep time: 15 minutes and 15 minutes for cooking

4 Serving

Ingredients:

- two cups brown rice, cooked
- one cup florets of broccoli
- 1 sliced bell pepper
- One carrot, thinly sliced
- 1 cup blanched snap peas
- Two tsp of soy sauce
- One tsp of sesame oil
- one tsp finely chopped ginger
- two minced garlic cloves
- Sunflower seeds as a garnish

Preparation:

1. Start by heating the sesame oil in a wok or large pan over medium-high heat.

2. Stir-fry the garlic and ginger for one to two minutes, or until fragrant.
3. Add the snap peas, carrot, bell pepper, and broccoli. Cook for five to seven minutes, or until the veggies are crisp-tender.
4. Toss the veggies with the cooked brown rice and soy sauce.
5. Cook the rice for a further three to five minutes, or until it is well warm.
6. Before serving, sprinkle sesame seeds on top.

Lettuce and Quinoa Salad Served with Lemon Vinaigrette

Description: This salad is full of nutrition and refreshing, with quinoa, chickpeas, and a tangy lemon vinaigrette. This recipe is ideal as a light supper or lunch.

20 minutes for preparation

4 Serving

Ingredients:

- One cup cooked quinoa,
- one can (15 oz) chickpeas,
- one cucumber, one cup cherry tomatoes,
- one halved red onion,
- one finely chopped 1/4 cup feta cheese,
- and one crumbled For garnish, use fresh parsley.
- A zesty vinaigrette
- Three tsp olive oil
- lime juice from one

- 1 tspn of mustard Dijon
- Add pepper and salt to taste.

Preparation:

1. Cooked quinoa, chickpeas, cucumber, cherry tomatoes, red onion, and feta cheese should all be combined in a big dish.
2. Combine the ingredients for the lemon vinaigrette in a separate small bowl.
3. After adding the vinaigrette to the salad, mix to thoroughly blend.
4. Serve cold, garnished with fresh parsley.

Millet and Vegetable Buddha dish:

Description: This filling dish is made with roasted veggies, creamy tahini sauce, and millet. This nutritious meal is a visual feast.

Cooking/Prep Time: 30 minutes for baking, 15 minutes for prep

Ingredients:

- one cup cooked millet
- One cup cherry tomatoes, one diced sweet potato, one sliced zucchini, and one
- one cup cooked chickpeas
- Two tsp of olive oil
- One tsp cumin
- One tsp of paprika
- Add pepper and salt to taste.
- Half a cup tahini

- lime juice from one
- two tsp of water

Preparation:

1. Set oven temperature to 400°F, or 200°C.
2. Add olive oil, cumin, paprika, salt, and pepper to the sweet potato, zucchini, cherry tomatoes, and chickpeas.
3. Bake the veggies and chickpeas for thirty minutes, or until they are soft and golden.
4. Layer roasted veggies and cooked millet to assemble the Buddha bowls.
5. To prepare the dressing, combine the tahini, lemon juice, water, salt, and pepper in a small dish.
6. Before serving, drizzle the Buddha bowls with the tahini dressing.

Risotto with Barley and Mushrooms

Description: Barley and mushrooms are cooked to a creamy perfection in this substantial and healthful spin on conventional risotto, making for a filling and healthy dinner.

Ten minutes are needed for preparation and forty minutes for cooking.

Ingredients:

- One cup rinsed barley, eight ounces sliced cremini mushrooms, one onion coarsely diced, and two minced garlic cloves
- 4 cups heated vegetable broth
- Half a cup of dry white wine, if desired

- Grated Parmesan cheese, half a cup
- Two tsp of olive oil
- Add pepper and salt to taste.
- thyme fresh as a garnish

Preparation:

1. warm the olive oil over medium heat.
2. Cook the chopped onion until it becomes tender.
3. Saute the sliced mushrooms with chopped garlic until the mushrooms release their moisture.
4. Add barley and heat, stirring, until just toasted, one to two minutes.
5. Pour the wine into the pan if using it, and heat it until it has largely evaporated.
6. One ladle at a time, start adding the heated vegetable broth and stir often until it is absorbed.
7. Keep doing this until the barley is cooked to your desired consistency and creamy.
8. Add the pepper, salt, and grated Parmesan cheese. Before serving, garnish with freshly cut thyme.

Roasted Vegetable Salad with Farro

This is a nutrient-dense salad with a blend of roasted veggies, balsamic vinaigrette, and farro. This is a tasty and hearty dinner.

Cooking/Prep Time: 30 minutes for baking, 15 minutes for prep

Ingredients:

- One cup cooked farro, one cup cherry tomatoes, one bell pepper cut in half, one zucchini chopped, one red onion sliced, and two tablespoons olive oil
- One tsp of dehydrated oregano
- Add pepper and salt to taste.
- balancing The vinaigrette
- Three tsp balsamic vinegar
- 1/4 cup of olive oil
- 1 tspn of mustard Dijon

Preparation:

1. Set oven temperature to 400°F, or 200°C.
2. Mix together olive oil, dried oregano, salt, and pepper and toss with cherry tomatoes, bell pepper, zucchini, and red onion.
3. Bake the veggies for 30 minutes, or until they are soft and golden.
4. Roasted veggies and cooked farro should be combined in a big dish.
5. To create the vinaigrette, combine the olive oil, Dijon mustard, balsamic vinegar, salt, and pepper in a small bowl.
6. Pour the vinaigrette onto the salad and mix thoroughly.

Sorghum and Black-Eyed Pea Bowl

This bowl, with a taste of the South, combines sorghum and black-eyed peas and is dressed with a tasty herb dressing. This filling dish is a visual feast for the senses.

Prep time: 20 minutes

Cooking time: 45 minutes

Portions served: two bowls

Ingredients:

- One cup of boiled sorghum
- One (15-oz) can washed and drained black-eyed peas
- 1 cup finely chopped collard greens; 1 shredded carrot; 1/4 cup finely chopped red onion
- Two tsp of olive oil
- One-third tsp apple cider vinegar
- One tsp honey and one tsp Dijon mustard

Preparation:

1. Cooked sorghum, collard greens, black-eyed peas, shredded carrot, and red onion should all be combined in a big dish.
2. To create the dressing, combine the olive oil, Dijon mustard, honey, apple cider vinegar, salt, and pepper in a small bowl.
3. Pour the dressing into the bowl, then toss to fully incorporate.
4. The dish of black-eyed peas and sorghum can be served cold or at room temperature.

Stir-fried vegetables with cauliflower rice

Description: This recipe, which substitutes cauliflower rice for regular stir-fry noodles and adds a vibrant assortment of veggies, is a low-carb and fulfilling meal.

Prep time: 15 minutes

Cooking time: 15 minutes

4 Servings

Ingredients:

- One head of cauliflower, finely shredded to resemble rice
- one cup florets of broccoli
- 1 sliced bell pepper
- One carrot, thinly sliced
- 1 cup blanched snap peas
- Two tsp of soy sauce
- One tsp of sesame oil
- one tsp finely chopped ginger
- Two garlic cloves and finely chopped sesame seeds as garnish

Preparation:

1. Put the cauliflower in a food processor and pulse until it resembles rice.
2. In a big skillet or pan,
3. Sesame oil should be heated at medium-high.
4. Add the garlic and ginger and stir-fry for one to two minutes, or until fragrant.
5. Add the snap peas, carrot, bell pepper, and broccoli. Cook for five to seven minutes, or until the veggies are crisp-tender.
6. Toss to mix. Add the cauliflower rice and soy sauce to the veggies.
7. Cook the cauliflower rice for a further three to five minutes, or until it is well warm.
8. Before serving, sprinkle sesame seeds on top.

Cranberry and Wild Rice Stuffed Acorn Squash

This meal, which is served inside roasted acorn squash, is a festive and hearty combination of wild rice and cranberry stuffing. The tastes of fall are celebrated in this dish.

Cooking/Prep Time: 45 minutes for baking, 20 minutes for prep

Ingredients:

- Two acorn squash, cut in half and seeded
- One cup cooked wild rice
- Dried cranberries, half a cup
- Two tablespoons of olive oil, 1/4 cup chopped nuts, and 1/4 cup sliced green onions
- A single tsp of dried thyme

Preparation:

1. Set oven temperature to 375°F, or 190°C.
2. Season with salt, pepper, and dried thyme after rubbing olive oil over the sliced sides of the acorn squash.
3. Squash halves should be placed cut side down on a baking pan and baked for thirty minutes.
4. Cooked wild rice, chopped nuts, dried cranberries, and sliced green onions should all be combined in a dish.
5. Stuff the wild rice mixture into each side of the squash when it has halfway cooked.
6. Bake the squash for a further fifteen minutes, or until it is soft.

7. Present the filled acorn squash as a delectable and nutritious dish.

Stir-fried veggies with Buckwheat noodles

This recipe, which replaces classic noodle stir-fry with buckwheat noodles and a colorful variety of veggies, is a tasty and healthy meal that is free of gluten.

Prep time: 15 minutes

Cooking time: 15 minutes

4 Serving

Ingredients:

- Eight ounces of buckwheat noodles, prepared as directed on the box
- one cup florets of broccoli
- 1 sliced bell pepper
- One carrot, thinly sliced
- 1 cup blanched snap peas
- Two tsp of soy sauce
- One tsp of sesame oil
- one tsp finely chopped ginger
- two minced garlic cloves
- Sunflower seeds as a garnish

Preparation:

1. Buckwheat noodles should be prepared as directed on the package, drained, and then left aside.

2. Warm the same oil in a wok or large pan over medium-high heat.

3. Stir-fry the garlic and ginger for one to two minutes, or until fragrant.

4. Add the snap peas, carrot, bell pepper, and broccoli. Cook for five to seven minutes, or until the veggies are crisp-tender.

5. Toss the cooked buckwheat noodles and soy sauce with the veggies.

6. Cook the noodles for a further three to five minutes, or until they are well warm.

7. Before serving, sprinkle sesame seeds on top.

These healthy grain substitutes come in a range of tastes and textures, giving you nutrient-dense meal options. Have fun trying out these recipes and adding them to your weekly meal prep!

Low-Oxalate Veggie Delights

Creamy Cauliflower Mash

A rich and velvety side dish that goes well with any dinner, this creamy cauliflower mash is a low-oxalate substitute for typical mashed potatoes.

15 minutes for preparation and 15 minutes for cooking

4 Servings

Ingredients:

- One big head of chopped cauliflower and two minced garlic cloves

- Twice as much unsalted butter
- 1/4 cup of thick cream
- Add pepper and salt to taste.
- Optional garnish: chopped chives

Preparation:

1. When cauliflower is fork-tender, steam or boil it.
2. Puree the cauliflower, butter, heavy cream, and minced garlic in a food processor until smooth.
3. If preferred, top with chopped chives and serve as a low-oxalate substitute for mashed potatoes.

Pesto with Zucchini Noodles

Description: This colorful and tasty pesto sauce combined with spiralized zucchini noodles makes a low-oxalate, gluten-free substitute for typical pasta meals.

15 minutes for preparation and 5 minutes for cooking

2 Servings

Ingredients:

- Four medium-sized spiralized zucchini
- One cup of fresh basil, raw
- Grated Parmesan cheese, half a cup
- 1/4 cup of almonds
- Garlic cloves, two
- Half a cup of virgin olive oil

Preparation:

1. Cut the zucchinis into noodles by spiralizing them.
2. Combine the garlic, pine nuts, basil, Parmesan, and food processor. Process till chopped coarsely.
3. Once the blender is operating, gradually add the olive oil and blend until the pesto is silky.
4. Add salt and pepper to taste and toss the zucchini noodles with the pesto sauce.

Brussels sprouts roasted in a lemon-tahini dressing

Description: This tasty, nutrient-dense side dish with a hint of tang from the lemon tahini dressing is made using oven-roasted Brussels sprouts that are low in oxalates

Ten minutes for preparation and twenty-five minutes for cooking

4 Serving

Ingredients:

- One pound of halved Brussels sprouts
- Two tsp of olive oil
- Add pepper and salt to taste.
- 1/4 cup lemon juice and tahini
- two tsp of water
- one minced garlic clove
- Add a garnish of sesame seeds (optional).

Preparation:

1. Set oven temperature to 400°F, or 200°C.

2. Add salt, pepper, and olive oil to Brussels sprouts and toss. Roast until crispy and brown, about 25 minutes.
3. To create the dressing, combine the tahini, lemon juice, water, and chopped garlic in a bowl.
4. Sprinkle the roasted Brussels sprouts with the lemon-tahini dressing, and if preferred, top with sesame seeds.

Primavera Spaghetti Squash

Savor a low-oxalate take on a traditional pasta meal, including a base of spaghetti squash combined with a rainbow of vibrant veggies in a delicate and herbaceous sauce.

Fifteen minutes for preparation and another fifteen minutes for cooking

4 Servings

Ingredients:

- One medium spaghetti squash that has been seeded and halved
- Two tsp of olive oil
- 1/4 cup chopped fresh basil, 1 cup halved cherry tomatoes, 1 cup sliced zucchini, 1 cup thinly sliced bell peppers, and 2 cloves minced garlic
- Add pepper and salt to taste.
- grated Parmesan cheese (optional) as a garnish

Preparation:

1. Set oven temperature to 375°F, or 190°C.
2. Roast the spaghetti squash halves for 35 to 40 minutes, with the sliced side down, or until they are fork-tender.

3. Tenderize the bell peppers, zucchini, cherry tomatoes, and minced garlic in a pan with olive oil.
4. Shred the cooked spaghetti squash with a fork to create "noodles" and combine it with the sautéed veggies.
5. Add the fresh basil and season with pepper and salt.
6. If desired, garnish with grated Parmesan cheese.

Salad with Cucumber and Radish

This light and crisp salad of cucumbers and radishes, topped with a light lemon vinaigrette, is a low-oxalate side dish that enhances the flavor of your meal.

Ten minutes of preparation.

Ingredients:

- Two cucumbers, cut thinly
- One bunch of finely cut radishes
- Two teaspoons of freshly chopped dill
- lime juice from one
- Three tablespoons pure olive oil

Preparation:

1. Add the chopped fresh dill, radishes, and cucumber slices to a bowl.
2. To make the vinaigrette, combine the lemon juice, olive oil, salt, and pepper in a small bowl.
3. Pour the lemon vinaigrette over the combination of radish and cucumber.
4. Toss lightly to coat, then serve right away.

Bell Peppers with Spinach and Mushroom Stuffing

Stuffed with a delectable mixture of spinach and mushrooms, these low-oxalate treats are not only tasty but also aesthetically pleasing.

Cooking/Preparation Time: 20 minutes cooking, 30 minutes baking

4 Serving

Ingredients:

- Four big bell peppers, seeded and halved
- Two cups of finely chopped mushrooms
- Two cups of freshly chopped spinach
- 1 cup of quinoa, cooked
- Half a cup of crumbled feta cheese
- One minced garlic clove and two tablespoons of olive oil

Preparation:

1. Set oven temperature to 375°F, or 190°C.
2. Sauté the spinach, mushrooms, and chopped garlic in a pan with olive oil until the mushrooms release their moisture.
3. The cooked quinoa, feta cheese, salt, and pepper should be combined with the sautéed mixture in a bowl.
4. Place a filling inside each half of a bell pepper.
5. Bake the peppers for thirty minutes, or until they are soft.

Stir-fried broccoli and almonds

Description: This low-oxalate meal, a simple and healthful stir-fry with broccoli and almonds, is a colorful and crunchy addition to your dinner table.

Ten minutes of preparation and ten minutes of cooking

Ingredients:

- 4 cups florets of broccoli
- Almond slices, half a cup
- Two tsp of sesame oil
- Two tsp of soy sauce
- One-tspn rice vinegar
- One tsp honey and one tsp grated ginger
- two minced garlic cloves
- Add a garnish of sesame seeds (optional).

Preparation:

1. Warm the same oil in a wok or large pan over medium-high heat.
2. Stir-fry the broccoli for 5 to 7 minutes, or until it becomes crisp-tender.
3. Stir-fry the almonds for a further three minutes after adding the slices.
4. Combine the soy sauce, rice vinegar, honey, grated ginger, and chopped garlic in a small bowl.
5. After adding the sauce, toss to coat the broccoli and almond mixture.
6. If desired, sprinkle sesame seeds over top and serve.

Cheese-topped cauliflower and broccoli bake

Description: A cheesy, cozy bake with broccoli and cauliflower, this low-oxalate recipe is nutritious and fulfilling.

Cooking/Prep Time: 20 minutes for preparation and 25 minutes for baking

6 Serving

Ingredients:

- One medium cauliflower, divided into individual florets
- two cups florets of broccoli
- One cup of cheddar cheese, shredded
- One cup of mozzarella cheese, shredded
- Grated Parmesan cheese, half a cup
- 1 cup of thick cream
- two minced garlic cloves

Preparation:

1. Set oven temperature to 375°F, or 190°C.
2. Broccoli and cauliflower should be boiled or steamed until barely soft.
3. Arrange broccoli and cauliflower in layers in a baking dish.
4. Heat the heavy cream, chopped garlic, and cheeses in a saucepan until the cheeses are melted and smooth.
5. Make sure the veggies are thoroughly covered before pouring the cheese mixture over them.
6. Bake for twenty-five minutes, or until bubbling and golden on top.

Garlic and Lemon Green Beans

Description: A low-oxalate side dish that goes well with any main course is made simply yet flavorfully with crisp green beans mixed in a zesty lemon garlic sauce.

Ten minutes for preparation and eight minutes for cooking

4 Serving

Ingredients:

- 1 pound of cleaned green beans
- Two tsp of olive oil
- two minced garlic cloves rind of one lemon
- lime juice from one
- Almond slivers as a garnish (optional)

Preparation:

1. Boil the green beans for 3–4 minutes to make them crisp-tender. Empty and place aside.
2. In a pan over medium heat, warm the olive oil.
3. Add the minced garlic and sauté it once fragrant.
4. In the skillet, combine the zest and lemon juice.
5. Green beans should be blanched and then well covered with the lemon-garlic dressing.
6. If preferred, garnish with slivered almonds and serve right away.

Flavorful and Nutrient-Packed Sides

Roasted cauliflower with turmeric

Improve the taste of your side dishes with this roasted cauliflower that has been flavored with turmeric. It adds color and minerals to every dish and is full of taste.

Ten minutes for preparation and twenty-five minutes for roasting

4 Serving

Ingredients:

- One head of chopped cauliflower
- Two tsp of olive oil
- One tsp of turmeric
- One tsp cumin
- One-half tsp paprika
- fresh cilantro to decorate

Preparation:

1. Set the oven temperature to 425°F (220°C).
2. Combine olive oil, paprika, cumin, turmeric, salt, and pepper with the cauliflower florets.
3. After spreading out on a baking sheet, roast the cauliflower for 25 minutes, or until it turns golden brown.
4. Before serving, garnish with fresh cilantro.

Stir-fried Quinoa and Vegetables

This vibrant and nutrient-dense side dish of stir-fried quinoa and vegetables is easy to prepare and a blast of flavors and textures.

Fifteen minutes for preparation and fifteen minutes for cooking

4 Servings

Ingredients:

- One cup of cooked quinoa
- Two tsp of sesame oil
- One cup of snap peas and two cups of chopped mixed veggies (carrots, broccoli, and bell peppers)
- three tsp of soy sauce
- One tsp of hoisin sauce
- one tsp finely chopped ginger
- two minced garlic cloves
- Green onions to decorate

Preparation:

1. In a wok or pan, heat the sesame oil over medium-high heat.
2. Stir-fry the snap peas and mixed veggies for five to seven minutes, or until they are crisp-tender.
3. Add the soy sauce, hoisin sauce, cooked quinoa, ginger, and garlic and stir. Simmer for five more minutes.
4. Before serving, sprinkle some chopped green onions on top.

Garlic in lemon Brussels sprouts roasted

Description: The vivid mix of lemon and garlic transforms Brussels sprouts into a zesty and tasty side dish. This roasted version is full of nutrients and tastes great.

Ten minutes for preparation and twenty-five minutes for roasting

6 Serving

Ingredients:

- One pound of trimmed and halved Brussels sprouts
- Two tsp of olive oil
- rind of one lemon
- two minced garlic cloves
- For garnish, use fresh parsley.

Preparation:

1. Set oven temperature to 400°F, or 200°C.
2. Add minced garlic, lemon zest, olive oil, salt, and pepper to Brussels sprouts.
3. Transfer to a baking sheet and bake for 25 minutes, or until well-done and golden.
4. Before serving, garnish with fresh parsley.

Spinach with Mushroom Quinoa Pilaf

A nutritious and tasty side dish, this nutrient-dense quinoa pilaf mixes earthy mushrooms, colorful greens, and aromatic herbs.

15 minutes for preparation and 20 minutes for cooking

4 Serving

Ingredients:

- One cup of washed quinoa
- Two cups of veggie broth and one spoonful of olive oil

- 8 oz. sliced mushrooms and 2 cups of fresh spinach
- two minced garlic cloves
- One tsp of fresh thyme

Preparation:

1. Combine the veggie broth and quinoa in a saucepan. After bringing to a boil, lower the heat, cover, and simmer the quinoa for 15 minutes, or until it is tender.
2. Warm the olive oil over medium heat.
3. Mushrooms are sautéed till golden brown.
4. Cook the fresh spinach in the skillet with the minced garlic, thyme, and oil until the spinach wilts.
5. Stir the cooked quinoa into the spinach and mushroom mixture. Add pepper and salt for seasoning.
6. Serve as a tasty and nutrient-rich side dish.

Sweet Potatoes Roasted with Garlic and Parmesan

Enjoy the ideal ratio of sweetness to savory with these tasty and nutrient-dense garlic Parmesan roasted sweet potatoes. They make a great side dish.

15 minutes for preparation and 30 minutes for roasting

4 Serving

Ingredients:

- Two big sweet potatoes, chopped and skinned
- Two tsp of olive oil
- three minced garlic cloves

- 1/4 cup of Parmesan cheese, grated
- A single tsp of dried thyme
- For garnish, use fresh parsley.

Preparation:

1. Set oven temperature to 400°F, or 200°C.
2. Add chopped sweet potatoes, olive oil, dried thyme, Parmesan cheese, and salt & pepper to a bowl.
3. After spreading out on a baking sheet, roast the sweet potatoes for 30 minutes, or until they are soft.
4. Before serving, garnish with fresh parsley.

Quinoa salad with Citrus and Herbs

This quinoa salad with citrus and herbs will add some color and brightness to your dinner. Full of herbs and fresh tastes, this is a low-calorie, high-nutrient side dish.

Fifteen minutes for preparation and fifteen minutes for cooking

4 Serving

Ingredients:

- One cup of washed quinoa
- Two cups vegetable broth One orange's zest and juice One lemon's zest and juice
- Two tablespoons of olive oil,
- 1/4 cup of freshly chopped mint,
- and 1/4 cup of freshly chopped parsley

Preparation:

1. Combine the veggie broth and quinoa in a saucepan. After bringing to a boil, lower the heat, cover, and simmer the quinoa for 15 minutes, or until it is tender.
2. Using a fork, fluff the quinoa and set aside to chill.
3. Combine the quinoa with the olive oil, salt, pepper, chopped parsley, chopped mint, and chopped lemon zest in a bowl.
4. Serve as a tasty and refreshing quinoa salad.

Herb and Garlic Roasted Mushrooms

Take your mushrooms to a whole new level with this side dish of roasted garlic and herbs. It's a straightforward yet sophisticated complement to any dish, bursting with delicious tastes.

Ten minutes of preparation and twenty minutes of roasting are required.

4 Serving

Ingredients:

- One pound of cleaned and halved mushrooms
- Three tsp olive oil
- four minced garlic cloves
- A single tsp of dried thyme
- One tsp of dehydrated rosemary
- For garnish, use fresh parsley.

Preparation:

1. Set oven temperature to 400°F, or 200°C.
2. Add salt, pepper, dried thyme, dry rosemary, and olive oil to the mushrooms.

3. After spreading out on a baking sheet, roast the mushrooms for 20 minutes, or until they turn golden brown.
4. Before serving, garnish with fresh parsley.

Carrots Roasted with Cumin Spice

Roasted carrots with a hint of cumin spice will give your dinner a blast of warm, earthy tastes. Full of nutrients, it's a vibrant, flavorful side dish.

Ten minutes for preparation and twenty-five minutes for roasting

4 Serving

Ingredients:

- One pound of peeled and sliced sticks of carrots
- A teaspoon of ground cumin and two tablespoons of olive oil
- half a teaspoon of coriander powder
- One-half tsp smoked paprika
- fresh cilantro to decorate

Preparation:

1. Set oven temperature to 400°F, or 200°C.
2. Combine olive oil, smoked paprika, ground cumin, ground coriander, salt, and pepper with the carrot sticks.
3. After spreading out on a baking sheet, roast the carrots for 25 minutes, or until they are soft.
4. Before serving, garnish with fresh cilantro.

Zucchini Noodles with Pesto

Take in the crispness of zucchini noodles dipped in bright pesto. This nutrient-dense, light side dish is a great substitute for classic spaghetti.

Fifteen minutes of preparation and five minutes of cooking

Ingredients:

- Four medium-sized spiralized zucchini
- Half a cup of cherry tomatoes
- 1/2 cup of fresh basil pesto
- 1/4 cup of roasted pine nuts
- Cheese Parmesan as a garnish

Preparation:

1. Turn zucchini noodles into spirals.
2. Zoodles should be sautéed for three to five minutes in a skillet until they are soft.
3. Add fresh basil pesto, toasted pine nuts, and cherry tomatoes.

Roasted Broccoli with Spices

This spicy roast broccoli will turn any broccoli into a mouthwatering side dish. It adds flavor to every dish and is full of nutrients and a hint of fire.

Ten minutes of preparation and twenty minutes of roasting are required.

4 Serving

Ingredients:

- Broccoli florets, 1 pound
- Two tsp of olive oil
- A single tsp of chili powder
- Half a teaspoon of chili powder
- 1 tsp powdered garlic
- slices of lemon as a garnish

Preparation:

1. Set the oven temperature to 425°F (220°C).
2. Add garlic powder, chili powder, cayenne pepper, olive oil, salt, and pepper to broccoli florets.
3. Arrange the broccoli on a baking sheet and bake it for 20 minutes, or until the edges start to crisp up.
4. Before serving, squeeze some lemon juice over the roasted broccoli.

Chapter 5: Decadent Desserts with a Twist:

Sweet Treats without the Oxalate Overload

Blueberry Lemon Chia Pudding:

A tasty and wholesome dessert, this blueberry lemon chia pudding mixes the zesty lemon flavor with the acidity of fresh blueberries to create a filling and low-oxalate treat.

Preparation/Cooking Time: 10 minutes for preparation and 4 hours for freezing

4 Serving

Ingredients:

- a single cup of blueberries
- Two tsp of chia seeds
- One cup of non-dairy milk, such as almond milk
- One tsp maple syrup
- rind of one lemon
- One tsp vanilla essence

Preparation:

1. Blueberries, chia seeds, almond milk, maple syrup, lemon zest, and vanilla essence should all be combined in a blender.
2. Mix until homogeneous.
3. Transfer the blend into containers or glasses and keep them chilled for a minimum of four hours or overnight.

4. Add some more blueberries and chia seeds as a garnish before serving.

Cookie Banana-Oat

Description: Enjoy a delightful chewiness without worrying about oxalate excess with these healthy Banana-Oat Cookies, which are naturally sweetened with ripe bananas.

Cooking/Prep Time: 15 minutes bake, 15 minutes prep

12 Cookies

Ingredients:

- One cup of old-fashioned oats, mashed with two ripe bananas
- Half a cup of almond flour
- 1/4 cup melted coconut oil
- One tsp vanilla essence
- half a teaspoon of cinnamon
- Optional: 1/4 cup dark chocolate chips

Preparation:

1. Adjust the oven temperature to 350°F (175°C) and place parchment paper on a baking pan.
2. Mashes the bananas and adds the oats, almond flour, melted coconut oil, cinnamon, and vanilla extract to a bowl.
3. If desired, fold in chocolate chips.
4. Spoonfuls of dough should be dropped onto the baking sheet and gently flattened.
5. **Bake for about 15 minutes, or until the edges are golden brown.**

Bits of Coconut-Lime Energy

These guilt-free Coconut-Lime Energy Bites are the ideal snack for a rapid energy boost since they have a natural sweetness and a burst of tropical flavor.

15 minutes for preparation

Ingredients:

- One cup of coconut shreds
- 1 cup almonds
- One cup of dates, pitted Two limes' zest and juice
- One tsp vanilla essence
- A dash of salt

Preparations:

- Shredded coconut, cashews, dates, lime zest, lime juice, vanilla essence, and a little amount of salt should all be processed in a food processor to produce a sticky dough.
- Shape the blend into small, palatable balls.
- Let it cool for a minimum of half an hour before serving.

Almond and Peach Tartlets

The delicious blend of sweet peaches and nutty almond tastes, all wrapped in a light and flaky crust, characterizes these Peach and Almond Tartlets.

Serving Quantity: Eight tarts

Cooking/Prep Time: 20 minutes bake, 20 minutes prep

Ingredients:

- Two peaches, cut thinly
- Almond flour, one cup
- One-fourth cup coconut flour
- 1/4 cup melted coconut oil
- Two tsp pure maple syrup
- One tsp almond extract
- A dash of salt

Preparation:

1. Warm up the oven to 350°F (175°C) and lightly oil a small tart pan.
2. Almond flour, coconut flour, maple syrup, melted coconut oil, almond extract, and a small amount of salt should all be combined in a bowl.
3. To make crusts, press the mixture firmly into the tartlet pan.
4. Place a layer of sliced peaches over each crust.
5. Bake until the edges are golden brown, about 20 minutes.

Raisin-Cinnamon Oat Bars

This recipe for Cinnamon-Raisin Oat Bars is a satisfying and wholesome snack that can be enjoyed as a sweet treat after a meal without worrying about consuming too much oxalate.

Size of Serving: 12 bars

Cooking/Prep Time: 25 minutes for baking, 15 minutes for prep

Ingredients:

- Two cups of traditional oats
- 1 cup of raisins
- Half a cup of almond flour
- One tsp of cinnamon
- 1/4 cup melted coconut oil
- 1/4 of a cup maple syrup
- One tsp vanilla essence

Preparation:

1. Adjust the oven temperature to 350°F (175°C) and place parchment paper in a baking dish.
2. Oats, raisins, almond flour, cinnamon, melted coconut oil, maple syrup, and vanilla extract should all be combined in a bowl.
3. In the baking dish, press the mixture firmly.
4. Bake till golden brown on top, about 25 minutes.
5. Let cool completely before slicing into bars.

Coconut-Mango Sorbet

Description: Savor the tropical richness of Mango-Coconut Sorbet, a dairy-free, refreshing treat that's simple to make and doesn't require oxalate overload worries.

10 minutes for preparation and 4 hours for freezing

6 serving

Ingredients:

- Three cups of frozen mango pieces
- One 14-oz can of coconut milk
- 1/4 of a cup maple syrup
- 1 lime's juice

Preparation:

1. Blend together frozen mango pieces, coconut milk, lime juice, and maple syrup using a blender.
2. Mix until homogeneous.
3. To get a smoother texture, stir the mixture every hour as it freezes in a shallow dish for at least 4 hours.
4. Pour into bowls and savor this deliciously tropical treat.

Berry and Vanilla Bean Parfait

Description: This visually beautiful and delectably sweet Vanilla Bean and Berry Parfait, free of oxalate issues, is made of layers of yogurt enriched with vanilla and fresh berries.

Size of Serving: 4 parfaits

15 minutes for preparation; no cooking is necessary.

Ingredients:

- two cups of yogurt
- One scraped vanilla bean (or one tsp vanilla essence)
- Two tsp of honey

- Two cups of mixed berries, comprising raspberries, blueberries, and strawberries

Preparation:

1. Combine the scraped vanilla bean seeds (or vanilla essence) and honey with the Greek yogurt in a dish.
2. Arrange a mixture of berries on top of the yogurt with vanilla in the serving cups.
3. Continue layering, then sprinkle some more honey over top.
4. For a delicious and light sweet treat, serve right away.

Avocado with Chocolate Mousse

Description: This rich and velvety Chocolate Avocado Mousse mixes the creamy texture of avocados with the richness of dark chocolate for a guilt-free treat.

Cooking/Preparation Time: 10 minutes cooking, 2 hours chilling

4 Serving

Ingredients:

- Two plump avocados
- 1/2 cup of cocoa powder without sugar
- half a cup of maple syrup
- One tsp vanilla essence One pinch of sea salt
- As a garnish, fresh berries

Preparation:

1. Avocados, cocoa powder, maple syrup, vanilla essence, and a small amount of salt should all be combined in a blender.
2. Blend till creamy and smooth.
3. Present the mousse made of chocolate and avocado in bowls, adorned with fresh berries.

Boiled Oatmeal Cups with Apple Cinnamon

These Apple Cinnamon Baked Oatmeal Cups are the ideal grab-and-go treat since they have a warm, soothing sweetness without causing oxalate overload.

Portion Size: Twelve Cups

Cooking/Prep Time: 25 minutes for baking, 15 minutes for prep

Ingredients:

- Two cups of traditional oats
- Half a cup of almond flour
- One tsp of cinnamon
- 1/4 cup melted coconut oil
- 1/4 of a cup maple syrup
- Two apples, chopped finely
- 1/4 cup of optionally chopped nuts

Preparation:

1. As you prepare a muffin tray, line it with paper liners and preheat the oven to 350°F/175°C.

2. Oats, almond flour, cinnamon, melted coconut oil, maple syrup, sliced apples, and chopped nuts, if used, should all be combined in a bowl.
3. Fill the muffin tray with a spoonful of mixture.
4. Bake till golden brown on top, about 25 minutes.

Muffins with lemon poppy seeds

Take pleasure in the spicy and light Lemon Poppy Seed Muffins, which won't make you worry about oxalate overdose.

Size of Serving: 12 Muffins

Cooking/Prep Time: 15 minutes cook time, 18 minutes bake time

Ingredients:

- two cups of almond meal
- One-fourth cup coconut flour
- One-half tsp baking soda
- A pinch of salt Two lemons' worth of zest and juice
- 1/4 cup melted coconut oil
- 1/4 of a cup maple syrup
- Three big eggs
- One-third cup poppy seeds

Preparation:

1. As you prepare a muffin tray, line it with paper liners and preheat the oven to 350°F/175°C.

2. Almond flour, coconut flour, baking soda, and a small amount of salt should all be combined in a bowl.
3. Combine the eggs, melted coconut oil, lemon zest, lemon juice, and maple syrup in a separate bowl.
4. After combining the dry and wet ingredients, fold in the poppy seeds.
5. A toothpick inserted into the muffin tray should come out clean after 18 minutes of baking.
6. Savor these deliciously sweet delights that are also considerate of people watching their oxalate consumption

Guilt-Free Indulgences for Health-Conscious Dessert Lovers

Avocado with Chocolate Mousse

Rich and velvety, this guilt-free chocolate mousse is prepared with avocados, which adds a creamy texture and rich flavor without sacrificing your health-conscious choices.

Ten minutes of preparation and no cooking are needed.

4 Serving

Ingredients:

- Two plump avocados
- 1/4 cup powdered cocoa
- 1/4 of a cup maple syrup
- One tsp vanilla essence One pinch of sea salt
- As a garnish, fresh berries

Preparation:

1. Transfer the flesh of the avocado to a blender or food processor.Mix in vanilla essence, maple syrup, cocoa powder, and a small amount of salt.
2. Blend till creamy and smooth.
3. After dividing into serving glasses, chill for a minimum of 60 minutes.
4. Before serving, garnish with fresh berries.

Banana Cookies with Oatmeal

Description: Ideal for fulfilling sweet cravings, these oatmeal banana cookies are naturally sweetened and chewy, making them a guilt-free treat for health-conscious dessert fans.

Size of Serving: 12 cookies

Ten minutes are needed for preparation and fifteen minutes for baking.

Ingredients:

- two ripe, mashed bananas
- Oats, rolled, one cup
- one-fourth cup almond butter
- 1/4 cup dark chocolate chips or raisins
- One tsp vanilla essence
- half a teaspoon of cinnamon
- A dash of salt

Preparation:

1. Adjust the oven temperature to 350°F (175°C) and place parchment paper on a baking pan.
2. Combine mashed bananas, almond butter, rolled oats, chocolate chips or raisins, cinnamon, vanilla essence, and a little amount of salt in a bowl.
3. Spoon dough onto the baking sheet in spoonfuls.
4. Bake until the edges turn brown, about 15 minutes.
5. Let cool completely before serving.

Parfait with Chia Seed Pudding

Description: A delicious parfait of chia seed pudding topped with granola and fresh fruit, this guilt-free dessert is a nutritious and visually pleasing meal for those who enjoy dessert but are also health-conscious.

Quantity served: two parfaits

10 minutes of preparation and 4 hours of chilling are required for cooking.

Ingredients:

- Half a cup of chia seeds
- Almond milk, one cup
- One tsp maple syrup
- One-half tsp vanilla extract
- Fresh fruit
- Oatmeal

Preparation:

1. Combine the almond milk, vanilla extract, maple syrup, and chia seeds in a bowl.

2. Stir occasionally and refrigerate for at least 4 hours or overnight.
3. Arrange granola and fresh berries on top of chia seed pudding in serving glasses.
4. Continue layering and put more berries on top.
5. Savor this parfait sans guilt.

Energy Balls with Coconut Dates

Description: Indulge your sweet craving guilt-free with these coconut date energy balls. Full of natural sweetness with a touch of coconut, they are a healthy dessert or snack option.

Twelve energy balls are served.

15 minutes for preparation; no cooking is necessary.

Ingredients:

- one cup of pitted dates
- cup of almonds
- 1/4 cup of coconut, shredded
- One-third cup chia seeds
- One tsp of coconut oil
- A dash of salt

Preparation:

1. Process dates, almonds, chia seeds, shredded coconut, coconut oil, and a small teaspoon of salt in a food processor until a sticky dough forms.
2. Form the dough into little spheres.

3. You might choose to coat the balls by rolling them in more shredded coconut.
4. Before serving, place in the refrigerator for at least one hour.

Apples Baked with Walnuts and Cinnamon

Description: These warm, cozy baked apples with walnuts and cinnamon provide a tasty, nutritious, guilt-free dessert choice.

Ten minutes are needed for preparation and thirty minutes for baking.

4 Serving

Ingredients:

- 4 apples, cut in half and cored
- One-third cup lemon juice
- One tsp of cinnamon
- 1/4 cup of walnuts, chopped
- Two tsp pure maple syrup

Preparation:

1. Turn the oven on to 375°F (190°C) and coat a baking dish with oil.
2. After arranging the apple halves in the baking dish, squeeze in some lemon juice.
3. Combine chopped walnuts and cinnamon in a small bowl.
4. Scatter the walnut-cinnamon mixture on top of the apples.
5. Pour some maple syrup on top.

6. Bake the apples for thirty minutes, or until they are soft.
7. Warm up and serve, topped with granola or a dollop of yogurt, if desired.

Dipped in Dark Chocolate Strawberries

These dark chocolate-dipped strawberries are a sophisticated and guilt-free dessert option for health-conscious dessert enthusiasts, offering a better take on a beloved pleasure.

16 strawberries per serving size.

Cooking/Prep Time: 15 minutes cook, 10 minutes rest

Ingredients:

- 16 fresh strawberries,
- 4 ounces of cleaned and dried dark chocolate,
- 2 tablespoons of melted chopped nuts, or optionally, shredded coconut

Preparation:

1. Use parchment paper to line a tray.
2. In a heatproof basin, melt the dark chocolate.
3. Each strawberry should be dipped into the molten chocolate, letting any excess drop off.
4. Transfer to the parchment paper and, if preferred, top with chopped nuts or shredded coconut.
5. Before serving, let it cool for a minimum of ten minutes in the refrigerator.

Yogurt Parfait with Almond Granola and Berries

Description: For health-conscious dessert enthusiasts searching for a delectable treat, this guilt-free yogurt parfait with fresh berries and almond granola is light and fulfilling.

Quantity served: two parfaits

Ten minutes of preparation and no cooking are needed.

Ingredients:

- two cups of yogurt
- One cup of mixed berries, including raspberries, blueberries, and strawberries
- Half a cup of almond granola

Preparation:

1. Arrange mixed berries on top of Greek yogurt in serving cups.
2. Over the berries, scatter the almond granola.
3. Turn the layers over.
4. Before serving, drizzle honey over the top.

Protein Smoothie Bowl with Mint Chocolate

Description: This mint chocolate protein smoothie bowl is a guilt-free way to indulge in a sweet treat while maintaining your health-conscious objectives. It's a light and protein-rich dessert choice.

Ten minutes of preparation

Ingredients:

- Two bananas, frozen
- 1 cup of leafy spinach
- Almond milk, one cup
- One serving of chocolate protein powder
- One-half tsp peppermint oil
- Add-ons: Almond slices, dark chocolate chips, and fresh mint leaves

Preparation:

1. Blend together frozen bananas, almond milk, chocolate protein powder, spinach, and peppermint extract in a blender.
2. Blend till creamy and smooth.
3. Transfer into bowls and garnish with sliced almonds, dark chocolate chips, and fresh mint leaves.

Chia Seed Popsicles with Raspberry

These guilt-free raspberry chia seed popsicles are a great way to cool off. Rich in fruity goodness and chia seeds, they're a great option for a cool, health-conscious dessert.

Size of Serving: Six Popsicles

10 minutes for preparation and 4 hours for freezing

Ingredients:

- Double-cup raspberries
- 1/4 of a cup maple syrup
- Two tsp of chia seeds
- One cup of coconut juice

Preparation:

1. Puree the raspberries, chia seeds, maple syrup, and coconut water in a blender until it's smooth.
2. Transfer the blend into popsicle molds.
3. Freeze until set, preferably for 4 hours.
4. Savor these juicy chia seed popsicles without feeling guilty.

Almond butter swirled banana nice cream

Description: A guilt-free substitute for regular ice cream, this rich and creamy banana nice cream with almond butter swirl is the ideal dessert for anyone watching their weight.

10 minutes for preparation and 4 hours for freezing

4 Serving

Ingredients:

- Cut four ripe bananas and freeze them.
- one-fourth cup almond butter
- One tsp maple syrup
- Measure 1 teaspoon of vanilla extract

Preparation:

- Frozen banana slices should be blended until creamy in a blender.

- Combine almond butter, maple syrup, and vanilla extract in a small bowl.
- Stir the mixture of almond butter into the nice cream made with bananas.
- After transferring, freeze for at least four hours in a container.
- Enjoy this guilt-free banana nice cream with a delicious swirl of almond butter by scooping it up.

Creative Low-Oxalate Dessert Hacks

Avocado Chocolate Mousse Parfait

Savor a decadent dessert free of guilt with this rich parfait made of avocado and chocolate. Avocado balances the amounts of oxalate while adding a silky texture.

Size of Serving: 4 parfaits

15 minutes for preparation; no cooking is necessary.

Ingredients:

- Two plump avocados
- 1/4 cup chocolate powder, unsweetened
- 1/4 cup maple syrup or honey
- One tsp vanilla essence
- A dash of salt
- Coconut cream whipped for stacking
- As a garnish, fresh berries

Preparation:

1. Avocados, cocoa powder, honey, maple syrup, vanilla extract, and a small amount of salt should all be combined in a blender. Mix until homogeneous.
2. Arrange the whipped coconut cream and avocado chocolate mousse in serving cups.
3. After layering again, add fresh berries on top.
4. Before serving, place in the refrigerator for at least one hour.

Lemon Poppy Seed Muffins Made with Coconut Flour

Description: A light and zesty treat ideal for sating your dessert cravings, these delectable muffins are made using coconut flour, a low-oxalate substitute.

Size of Serving: 12 Muffins

Cooking/Prep Time: 20 minutes for baking, 15 minutes for prep

Ingredients:

- One cup of coconut flour
- Half a cup of almond flour
- Half a cup of plain applesauce
- 1/4 cup melted coconut oil
- 1/4 cup maple syrup or honey
- Four big eggs.
- Juice and zest from two lemons
- One-third cup poppy seeds

- One tsp baking soda
- A dash of salt

Preparation:

1. As you prepare a muffin tray, line it with paper liners and preheat the oven to 350°F/175°C.
2. Combine the almond flour, coconut flour, eggs, honey, maple syrup, melted coconut oil, poppy seeds, lemon zest, lemon juice, baking soda, and a dash of salt in a bowl.
3. When a toothpick inserted into a muffin cup comes out clean, bake the batter in each muffin cup for 18 to 20 minutes.
4. Before serving, allow the muffins to cool.

Cauliflower Rice Pudding

This creative rice pudding replaces regular rice with cauliflower rice, offering a low-oxalate substitute without sacrificing its cozy, creamy texture.

Ten minutes for preparation and twenty-five minutes for cooking

6 Serving

Ingredients:

- three cups riced cauliflower
- Two glasses of almond milk without sugar
- 1/4 cup maple syrup or honey
- One tsp vanilla essence
- half a teaspoon of cinnamon powder
- 1/4 tspn of nutmeg

- A dash of salt
- Garnish with raisins (optional).

Preparation:

1. Cauliflower rice, almond milk, vanilla essence, cinnamon, nutmeg, honey or maple syrup, and a small amount of salt should all be combined in a pot.
2. Simmer for 20 to 25 minutes, stirring often, or until the cauliflower rice is soft and the stew thickens.
3. Before serving, take it off the stove and allow it to cool somewhat.
4. If desired, garnish with raisins.

Bars with Almond Flour, Berry Crumble

A low-oxalate take on a traditional favorite, these almond flour berry crumble bars have a delicious blend of a buttery crust, a layer of luscious berries, and a crumbly almond topping.

Size of Serving: 9 Bars

Cooking/Prep Time: 30 minutes for baking, 15 minutes for prep

Ingredients:

- Almond flour, one cup
- 60 ml of coconut flour
- 1/4 cup melted coconut oil
- 1/4 cup maple syrup or honey
- One tsp vanilla essence

- A dash of salt
- One cup of mixed berries, including strawberries, raspberries, and blueberries

Preparation:

1. Adjust the oven temperature to 350°F (175°C) and place parchment paper inside a square baking dish.
2. To make the crust, combine the almond flour, coconut flour, melted coconut oil, honey, vanilla essence, and a little amount of salt in a bowl.
3. Half of the crust mixture should be pressed into the baking dish's bottom.
4. Cover the crust with the mixed berries.
5. Scatter the leftover crust mixture onto the fruit.
6. Bake until the tops are golden brown, 25 to 30 minutes.
7. Let cool completely before slicing into bars.

Brownies with Zucchini and Almond Butter

Description: Try these brownies with zucchini and almond butter to sneak some vegetables into your dessert. They're rich, juicy, and a deft low-oxalate take on a traditional delicacy.

Size of Serving: 16 brownies

Cooking/Prep Time: 20 minutes for preparation and 25 minutes for baking

Ingredients:

- Grated zucchini in two cups, pressed to remove extra moisture

- One cup of butter almond
- Half a cup of maple syrup or honey
- Two big eggs
- One tsp vanilla essence
- one-third cup cocoa powder
- One-half tsp baking soda
- A dash of salt
- Chunks of dark chocolate as a garnish (optional)

Preparation:

1. Grease a square baking dish and preheat the oven to 350°F (175°C).
2. Grated zucchini, almond butter, honey, maple syrup, eggs, baking soda, vanilla extract, and a dash of salt should all be combined in a dish.
3. In the baking dish, distribute the batter equally.
4. If desired, garnish with bits of dark chocolate.
5. Bake for 25 minutes, or until a toothpick inserted into the center comes out slightly wet.
6. Let cool completely before slicing into squares.

Pumpkin Spice Chia Seed Pudding:

Savor the tastes of fall with this pudding made with pumpkin spice and chia seeds. This low-oxalate dessert recipe is filling and healthy at the same time.

Ten minutes of prep and four hours of cooling

4 Serving

Ingredients:

- 1 cup almond milk without sugar
- one-half cup pureed canned pumpkin
- Half a cup of chia seeds
- Two tsp pure maple syrup
- One tsp pumpkin spice mixture
- One-half tsp vanilla extract
- chopped nuts (optional) as a garnish

Preparation:

1. Almond milk, pumpkin puree, chia seeds, maple syrup, pumpkin spice blend, and vanilla extract should all be combined in a bowl.
2. To prevent clumping, let the mixture settle for a few minutes before whisking it once more.
3. For at least four hours or overnight, cover and chill.
4. Before serving, give it a stir and, if you'd like, top with chopped nuts.

Coconut Lime Sorbet with Low Oxalate

Description: Cool off with this delightful sorbet of coconut and lime. It's a straightforward, low-oxalate dessert choice that tastes wonderfully of the tropics.

Cooking/Prep Time: 30 minutes of stirring and 5 minutes of preparation

6 Serving

Ingredients:

- One 13.5-oz can of coconut milk
- Juice and zest from two limes
- Half a cup of maple syrup or honey

Instructions:

1. 1 teaspoon vanilla extract
2. Blend together coconut milk, lime juice, zest, honey, or maple syrup, and vanilla extract in a blender.
3. Mix until homogeneous.
4. Transfer the blend into an ice cream machine and process in accordance with the guidelines provided by the manufacturer.
5. To firm up, transfer to a jar with a lid and freeze for a few hours.
6. Enjoy this tropical sorbet by scooping it up.

Blueberry Almond Flour Mug Cake

This blueberry almond flour mug cake will quickly satisfy your sweet tooth. When you need a dessert that serves one, this is a simple, low-oxalate option.

Size of Serving: 1 Mug Cake

Five minutes are spent preparing and two minutes are spent cooking.

Ingredients:

- Almond flour, 1/4 cup
- One-third cup coconut flour
- One-fourth tsp baking powder
- A pinch of salt and one tablespoon of melted coconut oil
- two tsp of almond milk
- One spoonful of maple syrup or honey
- A quarter-tsp almond extract
- 1/4 cup blueberries, either frozen or fresh

Preparation:

1. Mix the almond flour, coconut flour, baking powder, and a small amount of salt in a cup that can be placed in the microwave.
2. Melt the coconut oil and stir in the almond milk, almond extract, honey, or maple syrup. Until smooth, stir.
3. Incorporate blueberries.
4. Cook in the microwave for 2 minutes on high, or until the middle is done.
5. Let cool a little before consuming.

Pieces of No-Bake Lemon Cheesecake

These spicy and creamy low-oxalate dessert bites are made without baking and have no added sugar. They are easy to put together and make a delicious, light dessert.

Meal Size: Twelve Bits

Cooking/Prep Time: 2 hours to chill, 15 minutes to prepare.

Ingredients:

- Almond flour, one cup
- 1/4 cup melted coconut oil
- Two teaspoons of maple syrup or honey
- 8 ounces of softened cream cheese
- 1/4 cup of powdered erythritol or desired sweetness
- One lemon's juice and zest
- One tsp vanilla essence

Preparation:

1. To make the crust, combine almond flour, melted coconut oil, and honey or maple syrup in a bowl.
2. To create crusts, press the mixture firmly into the bottom of a small muffin tray.
3. Beat cream cheese, powdered erythritol, lemon zest, lemon juice, and vanilla essence until smooth in a separate bowl.
4. Using a spoon, spoon the cream cheese mixture onto the mini muffin tin's crusts.

5. Chill for a minimum of two hours or until solidified.
6. The cheesecake bits should be carefully taken out of the micro muffin pan.
7. If desired, garnish with more lemon zest.
8. These delicious no-bake lemon cheesecake bites are best enjoyed cold.

Chia Seed Coconut Pudding Parfait

A gratifying and nourishing low-oxalate dessert choice is this chia seed coconut pudding parfait. This is a delicious delicacy made with layers of coconut yogurt and chia seed pudding.

Size of Serving: 4 parfaits

Ten minutes of prep and four hours of cooling

Ingredients:

- Half a cup of chia seeds
- Two cups of coconut milk without sugar
- 1/4 cup maple syrup or honey
- One tsp vanilla essence
- Double-cupped coconut yogurt
- As a garnish, fresh berries

Preparation:

1. Chia seeds, coconut milk, vanilla essence, and honey or maple syrup should all be combined in a bowl.
2. To prevent clumping, let the mixture settle for a few minutes before whisking it once more.
3. It should thicken into a pudding-like consistency after at least 4 hours or overnight in the refrigerator, covered.
4. Arrange the coconut yogurt and chia seed pudding in serving cups.
5. After layering again, add fresh berries on top.
6. Keep chilled until you're ready to serve.

These inventive low-oxalate dessert ideas come in a range of flavors and textures so you can indulge in delectable desserts without worrying about your oxalate intake.

Chapter 6: Revitalizing Drinks:

Hydration with a Purpose

The needs of the day frequently take precedence over staying hydrated in the hectic pace of modern life. But when you approach the process of hydration with intention, it becomes more than just a means of slake your thirst—it becomes an effective instrument. Let's explore the practice of "Hydration with a Purpose" and learn how consuming fluids intentionally may improve your mental and physical health and set you up for success.

Knowing the Significance of Hydration: Exceeding Thirst Hydration is essential to a healthy lifestyle since it helps with digestion, temperature regulation, and body function maintenance. But when one looks at it from the perspective of purpose, being hydrated becomes more than just a matter of survival; it becomes a deliberate act of self-care.

The Influence of Cautionary Drinking

1. Improving Mental Capacity:

Adequate hydration has been associated with greater cognitive performance, such as sharper focus, stronger memory, and higher levels of alertness. Maintaining proper hydration gives your brain the fluid it requires to operate at its best, which enhances mental acuity and sharpness.

2. Maintaining Physical Capacity:

Retaining optimal physical performance is contingent upon being hydrated, regardless of one's occupation or level of activity. Fatigue, cramping in the muscles, and a reduction in stamina can result from dehydration. Purposeful hydration guarantees that your body is well nourished for any obstacles that may arise.

3. Encouraging Mental Health:

Research indicates a clear connection between mood and hydration. A reduction in general wellbeing, anxiety, and irritability can all be caused by dehydration. By approaching water mindfully, you support not only your bodily well-being but also the development of emotional fortitude.

Drinking Routines for a Meaningful Life

1. Get Off to a Good Start:

Drink a glass of water first thing in the morning to boost your metabolism and start the day with intentional hydration.

2. Add Nutrients to Your Hydration:

Add intentional flavors to your water, such as mint, cucumber, or lemon. Not only does infused water taste better, but it also adds extra nutrients that are good for you.

3. Pay Attention to Your Body:

Pay attention to your body's cues. Although thirst is a sign, it's occasionally necessary to hydrate in advance. constantly have a reusable water bottle with you to guarantee that you are constantly hydrated.

4. Intentional Pauses:

Include quick stops for deliberate water intake throughout the day. These times not only help your body stay hydrated but also provide you a mental break that lowers stress and encourages awareness.

Oxalate-Conscious Smoothies and Juices

Oxalate-Light Berry Bliss Smoothie

This smoothie is tasty and low in oxalate, using low-oxalate berries that provide a taste boost without sacrificing nutrients.

Prep time: Ten minutes

2 Serving

Ingredients:

- One cup of frozen or fresh blueberries
- Half a cup of hulled strawberries
- half a cup of berries
- One banana
- One cup almond milk, or your preferred low-oxalate milk
- One-third cup chia seeds
- Cubes of ice (optional)

Preparation:

1. Blend together the almond milk, banana, strawberries, raspberries, and blueberries in a blender.
2. Mix until homogeneous.
3. Blend in the chia seeds once more until well combined.
4. If you'd like, add ice cubes and continue blending the smoothie until it reaches the consistency you like.
5. Pour into glasses and savor this oxalate-aware, antioxidant-rich treat.

Reviving Oxalate-Light Cucumber Mint Juice

This refreshing drink is a hydrating, low-oxalate juice made with refreshing cucumber and crisp mint.

Prep time: 15 minutes

2 Serving

Ingredients:

- Two cucumbers, cut and peeled
- 1/4 cup of mint leaves, fresh
- one juiced lime
- One spoonful of honey, if desired
- two cups water
- Cubes of ice (optional)

Preparation:

1. Cucumber slices, mint leaves, lime juice, honey (if used), and water should all be combined in a blender.

2. Mix until homogeneous.
3. If preferred, strain the juice to get rid of any pulp.
4. For an even more refreshing experience, pour over ice cubes.
5. Enjoy this oxalate-conscious, reviving beverage with a mint leaf garnish.

Oxalate-Friendly Pineapple Ginger Smoothie

This smoothie has a tropical vibe and is low in oxalate. It has ginger and pineapple for a spicy, anti-inflammatory kick.

Prep time: Ten minutes

2 Serving

Ingredients:

- two cups of raw pineapple cubes
- One banana
- One tablespoon of freshly grated and peeled ginger
- One cup of coconut juice
- One-half cup of low-oxalate yogurt
- One-third cup flaxseeds
- Cubes of ice (optional)

Preparation:

1. Blend together the grated ginger, banana, pineapple chunks, low-oxalate yogurt, coconut water, and flaxseeds in a blender.
2. Mix until homogeneous.

3. Pour into glasses, then enjoy this oxalate-conscious tropical treat.

Oxalate-Light Green Juice from Citrus Kale

This nutrient-dense green juice combines low-oxalate kale with the zesty qualities of oranges and lemons to create a reviving and oxalate-aware drink.

Prep time: 15 minutes

2 Serving

Ingredients:

- Two cups of chopped kale
- Two peeled and sliced oranges
- One lemon, sliced
- One peeled and sliced cucumber
- One tablespoon of mint leaves, fresh
- One-third cup chia seeds
- two cups water
- Cubes of ice (optional)

Preparation:

1. Kale, oranges, lemon, cucumber, mint leaves, chia seeds, and water should all be combined in a blender.
2. Mix until homogeneous.
3. If you would want a smoother texture, strain the juice.

4. For an even more refreshing experience, pour over ice cubes.
5. Raise a glass of nutrient-dense, oxalate-aware green juice.

Oxalate-Friendly Smoothie with Melon Medley

This refreshing, summer-inspired smoothie is made with a blend of low-oxalate melons and is light and nourishing.

Prep time: Ten minutes

2 Serving

Ingredients:

- One cup cubed cantaloupe, one cup cubed honeydew melon, one cup cubed watermelon, and one cup cubed low-oxalate yogurt
- One spoonful of honey, if desired
- One cup of coconut juice
- Cubes of ice (optional)

Preparation:

1. Put cantaloupe, watermelon, honeydew melon, low-oxalate yogurt, honey (if using), and coconut water in a blender.
2. Mix until homogeneous.
3. To add even more cold, add ice cubes.
4. Pour into glasses and savor this oxalate-conscious refreshing melon medley.

Oxalate-Light Green Juice from Spinach and Apple

This nutrient-rich green juice is made with low-oxalate spinach and apple crispness for a refreshing and oxalate-aware drink.

Prep time: 15 minutes

2 Serving

Ingredients:

- two cups baby kale
- two apples, peeled and cut
- Two cups of water, one cucumber, one lemon, and one tablespoon of fresh ginger, all peeled and grated.
- Cubes of ice (optional)

Preparation:

1. Put baby spinach, apples, cucumbers, lemons, gingers, and water in a blender.
2. Mix until homogeneous.
3. If you want the juice to have a smoother texture, strain it.
4. To provide even more refreshing flavor, add ice cubes.
5. Pour into cups and enjoy this green, oxalate-aware beverage.

Oxalate-Friendly Blueberry Basil Smoothie

This smoothie is distinct and tasty, combining the freshness and perfume of basil with the antioxidant-rich qualities of blueberries to create a wonderful oxalate-conscious drink.

Prep time: Ten minutes

2 Serving

Ingredients:

- One cup of frozen or fresh blueberries
- One-half cup of low-oxalate yogurt
- 1/4 cup of newly picked basil
- One banana
- One-third cup chia seeds
- One cup almond milk, or your preferred low-oxalate milk
- Cubes of ice (optional)

Preparation:

1. Blend together blueberries, banana, chia seeds, almond milk, fresh basil leaves, and low-oxalate yogurt in a blender.
2. Mix until homogeneous.
3. If desired, add ice cubes and mix one more.
4. Take note of the oxalate levels as you pour into glasses and savor this unusual blueberry and basil combination.

Oxalate-Light Carrot Orange Ginger Juice

Description: An energizing, oxalate-conscious beverage made with a zesty, nutrient-rich juice that combines carrots, oranges, and ginger.

Prep time: Ten minutes

2 Serving

Ingredients:

- 4 peeled and sliced carrots
- Three oranges, divided and peeled
- One tablespoon of freshly grated and peeled ginger
- One spoonful of honey, if desired
- two cups water
- Cubes of ice (optional)

Preparation:

1. Put the carrots, oranges, ginger, water, and honey (if using) in a blender.
2. Mix until homogeneous.
3. If you would want a smoother texture, strain the juice.
4. For an even more refreshing experience, pour over ice cubes.
5. Serve with an orange slice as a garnish and enjoy this energizing beverage that is low in oxalate.

Oxalate-Friendly Peach Almond Smoothie

This smoothie is velvety and oxalate-conscious, combining the sweetness of peaches with the nuttiness of almonds for a wonderful treat.

Prep time: Ten minutes

2 Serving

Ingredients:

- Two peaches, cut and pitted

- 1/4 cup unsalted almonds
- One-half cup of low-oxalate yogurt
- One spoonful of honey, if desired
- One cup almond milk, or your preferred low-oxalate milk
- Cubes of ice (optional)

Preparation:

- Sliced peaches, almonds, low-oxalate yogurt, honey (if used), and almond milk should all be combined in a blender.
- Mix until homogeneous.
- If desired, add ice cubes and mix one more.
- Pour into glasses, then enjoy this creamy peach-almond smoothie while being mindful of your oxalates.

Mango Coconut Oxalate-Light Smoothie Bowl

An oxalate-conscious breakfast or snack that combines the creamy smoothness of coconut with the lusciousness of mangoes in a tropical smoothie bowl.

Prep time: Ten minutes

2 Serving

Ingredients:

- Frozen mango chunks, two cups
- Half a cup of low-calcium coconut milk
- One-half cup of low-oxalate yogurt

- One banana
- Granola, sliced kiwi, chia seeds, and shredded coconut are the toppings.

Preparation:

1. Blend together frozen mango pieces, low-oxalate yogurt, banana, and coconut milk in a blender.
2. Mix until homogeneous.
3. Transfer smoothie mixture to bowls.
4. Add granola, sliced kiwi, chia seeds, and shredded coconut on top.
5. Savor this deliciously aware of oxalate smoothie bowl while keeping in mind its tropical ingredients.

Refreshing Beverages to Support Wellness

Citrus Mint Infused Water

This refreshing beverage helps you stay hydrated with a hint of citrus. Tastes good and is good for you because it's full of vitamin C and cooling mint.

Size of Serving: 1 pitcher

Cooking/Prep Time: 5 minutes; Chill Time: 2 hours

Ingredients:

- One orange,
- one lemon,
- one lime,
- one slice; fresh mint leaves;

- ice cubes Halite

Preparation:

1. Sliced orange, lemon, and lime should all be combined in a pitcher.
2. To taste, add more fresh mint leaves.
3. Pour water into the pitcher and add ice cubes.
4. Let the infusion sit in the fridge for a minimum of two hours.
5. For a zesty and minty experience, serve over ice.

Berry and Green Tea Smoothie

This antioxidant-rich green tea and berry smoothie will help you feel better. Rich in vitamins and minerals, it's a tasty approach to help your health.

Prep time: Ten minutes

2 Serving

Ingredients:

- One cup of brewed and chilled green tea
- One cup of mixed berries, including raspberries, blueberries, and strawberries
- One frozen banana
- half a cup of yogurt
- One spoonful of honey
- Cubes of ice (optional)

Preparation:

1. After brewing, let the green tea cool.
2. Blend together frozen banana, Greek yogurt, honey, mixed berries, and green tea in a blender.
3. Mix until homogeneous.
4. Pour into cups, then savor this superfood smoothie.

Cucumber Basil Sparkler:

This moisturizing cucumber basil sparkler will revive your senses. It's a health beverage that is spa-like, delicately sweetened, and filled with wonderful herbal flavors.

Ten minutes of prep and an hour of chilling are required for cooking.

2 Serving

Ingredients:

- One cucumber, cut thinly
- fresh leaves of basil
- One spoonful of honey
- One-third cup lemon juice
- carbonated water
- Cold cubes

Preparation:

1. Add the cucumber slices and fresh basil leaves to a pitcher.
2. Combine the lemon juice and honey in a small bowl, stirring to thoroughly blend.

3. Cover the cucumber and basil with the honey-lemon mixture.
4. Pour sparkling water into the pitcher and give it a little toss.
5. Before serving over ice, let it cool for at least one hour.

Ginger Lemonade with Turmeric

Take advantage of turmeric's anti-inflammatory properties by sipping this spicy turmeric ginger lemonade. A revitalizing drink that is cooling and calming.

Ten minutes of prep and an hour of chilling are required for cooking.

2 Serving

Ingredients:

- two cups water
- 1 tsp powdered turmeric
- One tablespoon of freshly grated ginger
- lime juice from two
- Two tsp of honey
- Cold cubes

Preparation:

1. Heat water, grated ginger, and turmeric in a saucepan until they begin to boil. Allow to cool.
2. Strain the mixture into a pitcher.
3. Stir the honey until it melts after adding the lemon juice and honey to the pitcher.

4. For at least one hour, let the lemonade cool.
5. For a golden and energizing drink, serve over ice.

Berry Hibiscus Iced Tea

Indulge in the lively tastes of hibiscus and berries with this cool tea. Rich in antioxidants, it's a tasty and nutritious option.

Cooking/Preparation Time: 10 minutes; chill for 2 hours

4 Serving

Ingredients:

- 4 bags of hibiscus tea
- Boil 4 cups of water.
- One cup of mixed berries, including raspberries, blueberries, and strawberries
- Two teaspoons of honey or agave syrup
- Cold cubes
- Garnish with fresh mint.

Preparation:

1. For five minutes, steep hibiscus tea bags in boiling water. Tea will cool when the tea bags are removed.
2. Blend together mixed berries and agave syrup in a blender.
3. Puree until smooth, then strain to get rid of the seeds.
4. Blend the chilled hibiscus tea with the berry purée.
5. Put the tea in the fridge to chill for a minimum of two hours.
6. Add some fresh mint as a garnish and serve over ice.

Fresca Pineapple Coconut Chia

Description: With this tropical pineapple coconut chia fresca, you can be more hydrated. Rich in chia seeds and electrolytes, it's a healthy and hydrating drink.

Cooking/Prep Time: 15 minutes; Chill Time: 1 hour

2 Serving

Ingredients:

- One cup juiced pineapple
- One cup of coconut juice
- Two tsp of chia seeds
- One spoonful of honey
- Slices of pineapple as a garnish
- Cold cubes

Preparation:

1. Pour the coconut water and pineapple juice into a pitcher.
2. Mix thoroughly after adding the honey and chia seeds.
3. Refrigerate the fresca for a minimum of 60 minutes.
4. Stir once more and pour over ice just before serving.
5. Slices of pineapple can be used as a tropical garnish.

Iced Latte with Minty Matcha

This minty matcha iced latte will energize your day with the power of matcha's antioxidants. a rejuvenating and pleasant drink.

Ten minutes of prep and an hour of chilling are required for cooking.

2 Serving

Ingredients:

- A couple of tsp matcha powder
- Two cups almond milk, or any other type of milk
- One spoonful of honey
- fresh leaves of mint
- Cold cubes

Preparation:

1. Mix the matcha powder with a tiny bit of boiling water in a bowl to make a paste
2. Mix almond milk, honey, and fresh mint leaves in a different pitcher.
3. Whisk the matcha paste into the almond milk mixture until thoroughly blended.
4. For at least an hour, chill the latte in the refrigerator.
5. For a minty matcha delight, strain the mixture and serve it over ice.

Fresca Watermelon Basil Agua

Description: Savor the refreshing agua fresca's herbal undertones and watermelon's moisturizing sweetness—it's the ideal summertime beverage.

Cooking/Prep Time: 15 minutes; chill for 2 hours

Ingredients:

- Four cups of diced watermelon
- 1/4 cup of newly picked basil
- Lime juice from two
- Two teaspoons of honey or agave syrup
- Cold cubes

Preparation:

1. Puree the watermelon and fresh basil leaves in a blender.
2. To get rid of the pulp, strain the mixture into a pitcher.
3. Stir thoroughly after adding the agave syrup and lime juice.
4. Let the agua fresca cool for a minimum of two hours.

Raspberry Mint Lemon Sparkler:

This pleasant and nutritious drink will help you stay hydrated with its vivid blend of raspberries, mint, and lemon.

Ten minutes of prep and an hour of chilling are required for cooking.

2 Serving

Ingredients:

- one cup of raspberries, raw
- fresh leaves of mint
- lime juice from two
- Two tsp of honey
- carbonated water
- Cold cubes

Preparation:

1. Muddle the mint leaves and fresh raspberries in a pitcher.
2. Stir in honey and lemon juice until the honey is dissolved.
3. Gently mix the sparkling water into the pitcher.
4. Before pouring the sparkler over ice, let it cool for at least an hour.\

Lemonade with Coconut Lavender.

This distinctive and delightful lemonade combines the tropical fragrance of coconut with the calming and fragrant tones of lavender.

Cooking/Prep Time: 15 minutes; chill for 2 hours

2 Serving

Ingredients:

- Cups four of coconut water
- 1/4 cup of lavender buds, dried
- Three lemons juiced
- Two teaspoons of honey or agave syrup
- Garnish with sprigs of lavender
- Cold cubes

Preparation:

1. Simmer the coconut water with the dried lavender buds in a saucepan.
2. Pour the coconut water flavored with lavender into a pitcher.

3. Mix thoroughly after adding the agave syrup and lemon juice.
4. Let the lemonade cool for a minimum of two hours.

For an elegant touch, serve over ice and garnish with sprigs of lavender.

Conclusion

It's not just the end of a book as we wrap up our culinary adventure with the "Toxic Superfoods Cookbook," but also the last leg of a revolutionary path toward recovery from oxalate overload and overall wellbeing. More than just a collection of recipes, this culinary guide is a monument to the efficacy of mindful eating and a wholistic approach to wellness.

Our goal has been clear from the outset: to provide people with a thorough resource that not only addresses the complexities of oxalate overload but also introduces a colorful and flavorful range of dishes into their lives. Every recipe acted as a nutritional ally, a means of rehabilitation, and a first step toward adopting a more wholesome, well-rounded way of life.

The flavors and nutrients woven throughout each recipe form the cookbook's heartbeat. We set out to transform how we think about food, starting with appetizers and ending with desserts, a journey where pleasure and healing come together. Its evidence that eating healthily doesn't have to be a chore; rather, it should be an appreciation of the wonderful diversity and energy that can be found in the world of low-oxalate ingredients.

These pages contain much more than just recipes; they also contain a plethora of information about oxalates, their health benefits, and the complex dance of flavors that can soothe and heal. All of the dishes are made with care and consideration for the special nutritional requirements that oxalate overload recovery requires because of the dedication to using only whole, low-oxalate ingredients.

Let us say goodbye to the "Toxic Superfoods Cookbook," but let this be the start of a lifetime journey towards holistic wellbeing instead of its demise. With a commitment to health, may the recipes found in these pages serve as the starting point of a path toward mindful eating, conscious living, and unwavering dedication.

I would like to conclude by sincerely thanking each and every reader who came along on this journey with us. The foundation of this cookbook is your dedication to wellness and discovery. I hope that the meals you've made become more than just filling food; they become acts of healing, acts of self-love, and signs of a life well lived.

Keep in mind that improving your health is a continuous process, and that every deliberate decision you make has the potential to do so. May the closing of this book serve as the beginning of a new chapter, where every meal presents a chance for recovery and every day represents a step closer to becoming a better, more energetic version of yourself.

Made in the USA
Las Vegas, NV
22 May 2024

90241572R00089